ALBERT CAMUS

A STUDY OF HIS WORK

ALBERT CAMUS

A STUDY OF HIS WORK

BY

PHILIP THODY

Assistant Lecturer in French
The Queen's University of Belfast

GROVE PRESS, INC. / NEW YORK

MANUFACTURED IN THE UNITED STATES OF AMERICA

TO MY WIFE

*The Author wishes to acknowledge his thanks
to Mr A. H. Terry for reading the manuscript
and to Mr W. H. Johnson for reading the proofs.*

CONTENTS

CHAPTER ONE

THE EXPRESSIONS OF THE ABSURD

IT was with the publication, in 1942, of *L'Étranger* and *Le Mythe de Sisyphe*, that Albert Camus changed quite suddenly from a little-known provincial essayist into one of the best-known French literary figures. This success is easily accounted for. His automatic assumption that life had no meaning, his denunciation of hope, his determined refusal of any comforting transcendence exactly fitted the mood of the time. Cataclysmic defeat had drifted into the monotony of occupation, the prospect of liberation seemed almost infinitely distant, and a philosophical view of the universe in which all paths to the future were rigorously closed and all optimism suppressed, corresponded exactly to the historical situation of the French people. *L'Étranger* (*The Outsider*) conveyed the atmosphere of the time before the philosophical essay *Le Mythe de Sisyphe* (*The Myth of Sisyphus*) offered an analysis of it and suggested a provisional attitude to be adopted. Both novel and essay had their origin in Camus's own personal thoughts and experiences, and the aptness with which they expressed the mood of 1942 was coincidence rather than deliberate intention on his part.

Meursault, the central figure of *The Outsider*, is characterized by his complete indifference to everything except immediate physical sensations. He receives the news of his mother's death merely with faint annoyance at having to ask for two days' leave of absence from the office where he works. At her funeral he has no sadness or regret, and feels only the physical inconveniences of watching over her body and following the hearse to the cemetery under the burning sun. He notes automatically and objectively everything which strikes his eye: the bright new screws in the walnut-stained coffin, the colours of the nurse's clothes, the large stomachs of the old ladies who had been his mother's closest friends, the whiteness of the roots in her grave. The day after the funeral he goes swimming, meets a girl whom he knows vaguely, takes her to see a Fernandel film and goes to bed with her that night. He shows no more affection or feeling for her than he had shown for his mother. When she asks him to marry her, he accepts with the calm remark that it is all the same to him. At his work, he is more interested in a detail like the pleasant dryness of a hand-towel at midday and its clamminess at night, than in a possible promotion and transfer to Paris. He becomes involved in a rather sordid affair with his next-door neighbour, in which he shows himself as indifferent to friendship and to the purely social convention of truthfulness as he was to love, and as a result of a series of accidents finds himself one day with a revolver in his hand, standing on a beach facing an Arab who is threatening him with a knife. Almost unconscious, under the blinding sun, of what he is doing, he shoots the Arab and then fires four more shots into his inert body. 'And it was like four sharp raps which I gave on the door of unhappiness.'[1]

In the second part of the book, until the very last page, Meursault remains as detached and indifferent as he was in the first. Inexplicably (to the ordinary reader) he never thinks of pleading self-defence when accused of the murder of the Arab, and, refusing to pretend to emotions he does not possess, expresses no remorse or feeling of guilt about his victim. The evidence of his insensitivity at his mother's funeral weighs overwhelmingly against him and he is condemned to death. The passivity with which he has greeted all that has happened suddenly breaks down at a visit of comfort which the prison chaplain makes to him. The chaplain's prayers and the consolation he offers of another life sting Meursault into a violent affirmation that this life alone is certain and that in it the inevitability of death obliterates all significance. The chaplain goes and Meursault is filled for the first time with 'the tender indifference of the world'. He realizes that he had been happy in his life, that he would like to live it all over again, and hopes, in order that all may be fulfilled, that there will be many people at his execution and that they will greet him with cries of hatred.

At any time the novel would have aroused considerable interest, for Meursault's experiences and his attitude towards them presented fascinating problems. Camus's skill of narration, the ease with which he alternated and contrasted his own personal lyrical style with a deliberate imitation of Hemingway's short, precise sentences, the mixture of annoyance and attraction with

death - creating affirmation of life.

---

[1] All notes and references are given at the end of the book.

which Meursault imposes himself upon the reader's mind, the violent satire of a world of justice in which a man is condemned for murder because he did not weep at his mother's funeral, all announced an author whose complexity demanded a further study in the fresh light provided by a work of exposition. The correspondence between Meursault's apathy and the hopeless atmosphere of 1942, and the explanation of this apathy in terms of the absurd in *The Myth of Sisyphus*, made Camus the recognized interpreter of a peculiarly contemporary state of mind.

Meursault is a man who, apparently quite unconsciously, accepts the premiss on which *The Myth of Sisyphus* is based. He recognizes, by the equivalent importance in his eyes of his mother's death and the annoyance of having to ask for two days' leave, the complete pointlessness of life and the 'deep lack of any reason for living' of which the essay on the absurd speaks. He illustrates, by his want of interest in all that happens, 'the senseless character of this daily agitation'. He believes in none of the things which normally give significance to life. Family affection, love, friendship, ambition, none of these has any meaning for him. Only the sensation of being alive either remains or seems to matter. Why should such a man not commit suicide? Why, above all, does he feel such an intense revolt when he is about to be killed? Why does the last page of the book introduce a theme of almost mystical communion with the world which nothing in Meursault's character had previously announced? These are the questions to which *The Myth of Sisyphus* suggests an answer. The problem of suicide, writes Camus in the opening sentence of *The Myth of Sisyphus*, is the only really serious philosophical problem. Is suicide a necessary consequence of the recognition that life has no meaning? 'Does the absurd demand that I should kill myself?—this problem must be accorded precedence over all others.' Camus's study of the human predicament begins with a *tabula rasa* of all certainties. The basic question of whether we should be alive at all must be answered before any attempt is made to establish value or morality.

Camus enumerates the various ways in which the absurd manifests itself: we are all exposed to its effects and Camus himself is so conscious of it that he assumes rather than explains its existence. Our train of thought may be broken, our companion may ask us what we are thinking of, and, suddenly conscious that our mind was completely empty, we are aware of 'this singular state of mind where absence becomes eloquent ... ' which may be the first revelation of the absurd. Suddenly, in the midst of the normal monotony of life, we stop to ask why and our existence becomes—like that of Meursault—'a weariness tinged with amazement'. The world shows itself bleak, hostile and unknowable and we do not recognize ourselves in the looking-glass. Above all, we are suddenly aware of our own mortality and, writes Camus, 'no morality and no effort can be justified *a priori* in face of the bloodstained mathematical certainties which dominate the human lot'. This consciousness of inevitable death is the most overpowering emotional evidence of the absurd and seems to have been at the basis of Meursault's experience. An examination of the intellectual manifestations of the absurd, however, reveals more clearly its true nature. We can never satisfy our longing for absolute knowledge, for science can do no more in the way of explaining the world than enumerate phenomena and describe them by images. By way of illustration, Camus quotes the example of the modern physicist who tries to explain matter in terms of the electronic theory, but is finally obliged to admit that no real and rational explanation can be given. It is from the clash between our desire for complete explanation and the essential opacity of the world that the absurd is born. But this is a new piece of evidence, and begins a fresh stage in the analysis of the absurd.

To say that the world itself is absurd is to anticipate and to affirm something which no argument can as yet justify. In itself, the world can be neither absurd nor reasonable, since it is only man's mind which introduces the concept of reason by which, since it does not conform to it, the world can be judged absurd. The absurd can occur only when two elements are present—the desire of the human mind that the world should be explicable in human terms, and the fact that the world is not thus explicable. 'What is absurd,' writes Camus, 'is the clash between its irrationality and the desperate hunger for clarity which cries out in man's deepest soul. The absurd depends as much upon man as upon the world. For the time being, it is their only link.' The absurd, like the Cartesian *cogito*, is the first result of thinking about the world and about ourselves. It results from the conflict between our awareness of death and our desire for eternity, from the clash between our demand for explanation and the essential mystery of all existence. In the present age, when rationalism has so often been shown to be an inadequate principle of explanation, this experience of the world has been widely shared. What, asks Camus, has been the reaction of thinkers towards it, and how have they replied to the first question which it poses, that of suicide? Have Dostoievsky, Kierkegaard, Kafka, Chestov, Husserl and Jaspers reached any valid conclusions as to the attitude to be adopted towards the absurd? A review of the solutions which their philosophies offer to the problem is the third stage in the argument which leads Camus towards his answer.

None of them, he immediately perceives, has been faithful to it and maintained it in its true position as the *unique donnée*. If none commits suicide, thus removing its original cause, which was the intrusion of the human mind, all find some other way of destroying it. All become reconciled to the irrationality of the world and consent to see man's demand for the reasonable refused and his intellect humiliated. All take the rationally un-justifiable leap which enables them to transcend the antinomy between man and the world, and destroy the real tension of the absurd. Jaspers and Kierkegaard deify the absurd, Chestov identifies it with God, and all three thinkers, whatever their other differences, unite in worshipping the incomprehensible because of its mystery. Husserl and the phenomenologists illogically find absolute value in individual things, and thus restore the principle of explanation whose absence was at the very origin of the absurd. Camus refuses to follow these thinkers in their unjustifiable leap into reconciliation. It is because the universe is not explicable in human terms that the absurd exists. To offer, as a solution to the problem which it creates, an explanation of the universe which is by definition beyond the reach of human reason is unjustly to dismiss the absurd by altering the nature of the problem. 'For the absurd mind,' writes Camus in one of the phrases whose clarity and intensity mark him out as a writer among philosophers, 'reason is useless and there is nothing beyond reason.' Camus adopts, on the plane of knowledge, the same refusal to accept that which is beyond his understanding as he will assume later towards the problem of suffering. He is already *l'homme révolté*, the rebel who justifies man and refuses an inhuman world.

The same intellectual rigour which caused Camus to criticize irrational evasions of the absurd also brings him to reject physical suicide. Human destiny, with all its contradictions, must be accepted as it is and life must be lived in accordance with this acceptance. 'Now man will not live out his destiny, knowing it to be absurd, unless he does everything to keep present in his mind the absurdity which his consciousness has revealed. To deny one of the terms of this opposition is to escape from it. ... Living consists of keeping the absurd alive. Keeping it alive is essentially a question of looking at it. Unlike Eurydice, the absurd dies only when one looks away.' In his first important piece of philosophical writing, Camus exalts the value of consciousness which is one of the oldest parts of the humanist tradition. Although Meursault seems to be above all lacking in awareness, he is nevertheless living out his absurd destiny in accordance with the ideas which Camus expresses in *The Myth of Sisyphus*. He reveals his reasons only at the very end of the book. His apathy is justified in his outburst of refusal of the chaplain's prayers. 'Nothing, nothing at all had any meaning and I knew why. He knew why as well. From the far off depths of my future, during the whole of this absurd life that I had led, a dark breath rose towards me, blowing through the years which had not yet come, bringing with it an equal insignificance to the no more real years that I was living through. What did other people's death matter, what did love for my mother matter, what did his god matter, what did the choice between different lives matter, since one fate would single me out and together with me the thousand million others who, as he did, said they were my brothers?' For Meursault the absurd is essentially the result of his awareness of his own mortality, of the 'bloodstained mathematics which dominate the human lot'. He is the 'everyday man' described in *The Myth of Sisyphus* who, before his consciousness of the absurd, had projects, hopes, ambitions, the belief that he was free to order his life, but who has realized that 'all that is disproved in one breathtaking sweep by the absurdity of a possible death'.

Meursault's apathy and indifference to the normal reasons for living were thus explained by one aspect of the idea of the absurd which Camus expressed in *The Myth of Sisyphus*. Further light was thrown upon his reasons for remaining alive and the nature of his final revolt against death by the development of Camus's arguments. The absurd frees man from all feeling of responsibility, annihilates the future and leaves only one certainty—the sensation of being alive. The question is now, not to live well in a moral sense—for the absence of moral rules renders this meaningless—but *vivre le plus*, replace the quality of experiences by their quantity. At first sight Meursault seems a very poor example of the absurd man. For whereas in *The Myth of Sisyphus* Camus describes three men—the actor, the seducer and the conqueror—who by the nature of their lives illustrate 'the passion to exhaust everything which is given'—or, expressed in more vulgar terms, to get the most out of life—he creates in Meursault a character remarkable for his apparent lack of passion. Yet Meursault has his own *morale de la quantité* which is equal to that of the most versatile actor or the most energetic conqueror. It was partly for aesthetic reasons— a work of imagination must not be too close an illustration of a work of reasoning—partly because Meursault already existed as an autonomous character in his mind, and essentially because of a certain taste for irony and mystification, that Camus made his outsider not a conqueror, an actor or a Don Juan, but a clerk in an office. He wished to show that the three types of man whom he described were not the only ones to which a philo- sophy of the absurd could give rise, and that his essay was essentially an exploration of a certain kind of experience, rather than an attempt to lay down fixed attitudes. The clue to the real relationship between *The Myth of Sisyphus* and *The Outsider* is to be found in the phrase in the essay where Camus says that 'a temporary employee at the Post Office is the equal of a con- queror if he has the same consciousness of his fate'. Meursault has recognized the absurdity of life and has gone through the experience of the absurd before his story begins. His lack of consciousness is only apparent—at several points of the story he shows himself a shrewd observer of men and society—and is partly the result of a technique of narration which seeks to represent a universe entirely devoid of order and significance. Meursault, although an outsider in society and a stranger to himself, is by no means completely indifferent to the world. His domain is the physical life. To swim, to run, to make love, to feel the sun on his face, to walk through Algiers in the cool of the evening—it is these experiences which have given him happiness and which make him wish to live the same life again. His indifference is not towards life itself but only towards those emotions to which society, living on the dead belief that the world is reasonable and significant, attributes an arbitrary importance. He is the outsider who refuses to play the game of society because he sees the emptiness of the rules, and his failure to conform causes society to will his death. His last desire—'the final thing I had to hope for was that there would be crowds of people waiting for me on the morning of my execution and that they would greet me with cries of hatred'—expresses a revolt against this society and a scorn for its conventions. In the pantheism of the closing pages—'As if this great rage had purged me of evil, emptied me of hope, in front of this night heavy with signs and with stars, I opened myself for the first time to the tender indifference of the world'—the cult of the physical life which has been latent throughout the novel comes to the surface. The passage corresponds to the description, at the end of *The Myth of Sisyphus*, of the immense importance which pure physical existence assumes for Sisyphus as he prepares, once again, to push his stone to the top of the hill. 'Each of the specks on this stone, each glint of light on the surface of this mountain shrouded in night, is a universe in itself. The fight towards the summit is in itself sufficient to satisfy the heart of man. We must imagine Sisyphus as happy.' Both Sisyphus and Meursault— the proletarian of the Gods and the proletarian of modern society—are at one and the same time both happy and unreconciled. In the different versions of the myth of Sisyphus, Camus finds that he is always characterised by his 'scorn for the Gods, his hatred of death and his passion for life'. These are qualities which can also be found in Meursault. Far from inviting his readers to a *delectatio morosa* in their own hopeless condition, Camus found that the absurdity of the world was, paradoxically, an invitation to happiness.

It was here that his originality lay. In making the absurd the centre of his preoccupations he was dealing with a problem which had been popularized by thinkers before being made acute by everyday life. As early as 1926 André Malraux had dealt quite fully with it in his *La Tentation de l'Occident* and had made of Garine, the hero of *Les Conquérants*, a man who rejected normal society because of its absurdity in his eyes. In 1938 Sartre's *La Nausée* had been almost entirely devoted to the expression of the absurdity of all existence. The thinkers whom Camus discussed in *The Myth of Sisyphus* were well-known, at least in philosophical circles, before the war. Camus neither invented the absurd nor introduced it into France. Wishing to express his own views on life in a fashionable manner he chose to write a philosophical novel and an essay on the absurd. By studying the way in which other writers on the absurd abandon their revolt and become reconciled, he confirmed his own instinctive rejection of any value that would deprive his life of its full tragic intensity. He used the example of other thinkers, as he was to do in *L'Homme révolté*, in order to make his own ideas stand out more clearly by contrast. 'One finds one's way,' he writes, describing his own technique, 'by discovering the paths which lead away from it.' The writers examined in *The Myth of Sisyphus* show how difficult it is to maintain the tension of refusal demanded by the absurd. As far as Camus's own thought was concerned there was nothing essentially new in *The Myth of Sisyphus*. It was a coincidence between the ideas which Camus had already expressed in his early lyrical essays and the climate of opinion in the early 1940's that made Claude Mauriac describe *The Myth of Sisyphus*, in retrospect, as 'a revelation and the putting into order of the spiritual confusion in which, like most young men of my age, I then found myself' *The Myth of Sisyphus* was for Camus the intellectual justification in the context of contemporary philosophy of what he had instinctively felt and expressed in *L'Envers et l'Endroit* and *Noces*. It is because life ends so completely in death, and because there is no transcendence to give it significance, that its price is infinite. This is the central thought in both *The Myth of Sisyphus* and in Camus's early essays. It is not mere coincidence that, bathed about as he was by the atmosphere of the Mediterranean, Camus should have put at the beginning of *The Myth of Sisyphus* the same quotation which heads Valéry's *Le Cimetière marin*. 'Oh my soul, seek not after immortal life, but exhaust the fullness of the present.'

Camus was born in 1913 in the small town of Mondovi in Algeria. His father was killed in the first world war and Camus was brought up by his mother in a home which, described in *L'Envers et l'Endroit* (*Betwixt and Between*), appears sordid and poverty-stricken. These first essays published in 1936 already show the quality which will run through the whole of Camus's early work. There is, on the one hand, the misery of man, and on the other 'all the light of the world'. 'I am linked with men by all my pity and my gratitude, with the world by all my acts,' he wrote. 'Between these two opposites I do not want to choose, and I do not like a choice to be made.' He is torn between his love for his fellow creatures and his ability to forget them in an instinctive communion with the world. 'And when am I more true to myself than when I *am* the world?' he writes, feeling the temptation to forget humanity in this complete pantheistic absorption and loss of personality. But, he recognizes, this is not possible. He must remain lucid and ironic, be conscious of the essential tragedy of existence, realize that 'there can be no love of living without despair of life'. The world is surprisingly simple in its tragedy, so simple that man alone introduces any complexity that there is. It is honest to avoid complicating issues and instead state things exactly as they are. 'Don't let them tell you any stories. Don't let them tell you of the man condemned to death that he has "paid his debt to society", but "they're going to chop his head off"'. It seems nothing at all. But it does make a bit of difference all the same. And after all, there are people who prefer to look their fate in the eyes.' This refusal to admit anything but the world's simplicity becomes one of Meursault's main characteristics. He is, from this point of view, an exemplary character whose complete honesty a Pharisaic society finds unbearable. *Betwixt and Between* gives the feeling of the absurd which *The Myth of Sisyphus* expresses in more systematic terms. *The Myth of Sisyphus* begins with a particular example of the suicide of a man who had killed himself because a friend had spoken to him in an indifferent tone of voice. This example is taken directly from *Betwixt and Between* and is, for Camus, a symbol of the world's simplicity. 'And if you really want to give a reason, he killed himself because a friend spoke to him in an indifferent tone of voice. Thus, every time that I have been given the chance to understand the profound meaning of the world, I have always been astounded by its simplicity.'

The reasons for rejecting the suicide which is such a simple thing in an absurd world are given full poetic expression in Camus's second collection of essays, *Noces* (*Nuptials*). The development of ideas in *The Myth of Sisyphus*, from the realization that the world is absurd to the determination to draw from its absurdity a greater intensity of experience, mirrors almost exactly the transition from *Betwixt and Between* to *Nuptials*.

There are two sides to the absurd in Camus's early work, the dark and the light, and this duality is announced in his first essays.

'One does not discover the absurd,' he wrote in *The Myth of Sisyphus*, 'without being tempted to write a manual of happiness.' *Nuptials* was this manual, and the intensity of physical joy which it describes increases the awareness of the absurd. 'Everything which exalts life at the same time increases its absurdity. In the summer of Algeria I learn that only one thing is more tragic than suffering and that is the life of a happy man. But this too can lead to a greater life, since it can teach us not to cheat.' Mortality in a meaningless world infinitely increases the value of life. All the complicated reasoning of *The Myth of Sisyphus* did no more than confirm this instinctive knowledge. The complete absence of significance of life which Meursault incarnates, and his awareness of life's importance on a physical plane, are what Camus himself felt at Djémila. 'What meaning have words like "future", "improvement" or "position"? What do people mean by "the progress of the heart"? If I obstinately refuse all the "later on" of this world, it is because I do not want to give up my present riches.' *Betwixt and Between* introduced Meursault's cruel lucidity. *Nuptials* expresses the joys which made his life worth living and which he regrets as he lies in his prison cell waiting to see whether his appeal will be allowed. The feel of the sun, the cry of the boys selling iced drinks in the square, the pleasures of swimming and walking on the beach, the cool of the evening and the sudden dusk of Mediterranean countries— these are the pleasures which Camus describes in *Nuptials* and they are a very personal element in Meursault's character. The one moral principle which persists in Meursault after the disappearance of all other values is something which Camus admires in the simple pagan civilization of North Africa. It is the quality of manliness, the observance of certain simple rules which society has not incarnated in its laws and which Meursault gains no credit for having observed. The feeling of communion of man with the world to which Camus cannot, for reasons of artistic consistency, give full expression in *The Outsider* and *The Myth of Sisyphus*, nevertheless dominates his final attitude. It is evident in the sensuality of the prose of *Nuptials*, in the yearning for a closer contact between man and the world. The theme of the book is expressed in one of its most representative images:

'I must be naked and plunge into the sea, the scents of the earth still about me, wash off these scents in the sea, and consummate on my own flesh the embrace for which, lips to lips, earth and sea have for so long been sighing.' It is because Camus, unlike Kafka, Kierkegaard and Sartre, feels instinctively that although the world may at times appear indifferent and strange, he is basically at home in it on the physical plane, that all his logic leads to a rejection of suicide. It is because he feels satisfied with his own world—'Not that one should behave as a beast, but I can see no point in the happiness of angels'—that he refuses all transcendence and all belief which creates a value other than the physical life. The condemnation of *l'esquive*, of the failure to confront reality as it is which he finds in the Existentialist thinkers is an instinctive emotional movement on his part. At Djémila, after his refusal of 'all the "later on" of this world' he goes on: 'I do not want to believe that death opens out onto another life. For me it is a closed door. I do not say that it is a "step we must all take" but that it is a horrible and dirty adventure. All the solutions which are offered to me try to take away from man the weight of his own life. And, watching the heavy flight of the great birds in the sky at Djémila, it is exactly a certain weight in my life that I ask for and that I receive ... I have too much youth in me to speak of death. But if I did speak of it, it is here that I should find the precise word which would, midway between horror and silence, express the conscious certainty of a death without hope.' This spiritual and material climate of North Africa dominates the philosophical climate of *The Myth of Sisyphus* and constitutes the principal difference which distinguishes Camus from Sartre or Kierkegaard or even Malraux as a philosopher of the absurd.

The particular kind of absurdity of *The Myth of Sisyphus* is not however the only one with which Camus is concerned. *The Outsider* is a complex work and contains, in addition to a kind of Rousseauistic condemnation of society, two distinct ideas of the absurd. There is first of all the essential lack of coherent significance in the world. This is communicated to the reader by the style in which the novel is written and by Meursault's attitude to his experience. Sartre, in his *Explication de 'L'Étranger'*, found that the short unanalytical, descriptive phrases expressed a vision of the world from which all attribution of order was absent. This absurdity is incarnated in Meursault's apathy and

attitude towards life. His tragic fate adds a second absurdity to
the first. Meursault's condemnation is absurd—or is made to
appear absurd by the emphasis which Camus gives to certain
aspects of the story at the expense of others—because society
and its rules are absurd. Or rather, because society incarnates a
malign, ontological absurdity which prevents Meursault from
continuing to be happy. Meursault is condemned through a
misunderstanding. It is not because he killed the Arab but
because he had not wept at his mother's funeral that he is executed. The die is loaded against man and the nature of the world
is such that he can build nothing on his happiness. This is
emphasized in the story which Meursault finds in a newspaper
cutting which had slipped between the mattress and the wooden
bed in his cell. A man left his native village in Czechoslovakia,
made his fortune and married, and returned twenty-five years
later to the village where his mother and sister kept an inn. They
did not recognize him and, as a joke, he asked them to give him
a room without telling them who he was. That night his mother
and sister murdered him in order to rob him—as they did all
travellers—and threw his body into the river. His wife came to
look for him next morning and revealed who he was, with the
result that both his mother and sister killed themselves. Meursault found the story unbelievable from one point of view but,
from another, quite natural. It is in a way a symbol of Meursault's own fate. The absurdity of the world is not merely
passive, the logical result of a consciousness of inevitable death
and of the absence of values, it is also a cruel and hostile force.
The Myth of Sisyphus gives no expression to this kind of absurdity. Camus's two plays, *Le Malentendu* and *Caligula*, produced
in 1944 and 1945, lay emphasis on this other and less optimistic
face of the absurd.

The plot of *Le Malentendu* (*Cross-Purpose*), with one or two
modifications, is the plot of the story which Meursault found in
his cell. The most important change is the reason why the
traveller, Jan, does not reveal his identity. He wishes to be recognized and find his home. He tells his wife: 'One cannot always
remain an outsider; a man needs happiness, it is true, but he also
needs to find his place in the world.' Not everyone can adopt the
attitude of Meursault and remain an outsider, indifferent to the
world. But Jan's desire to be recognized, his search for a universe
in which he will be at home, ends as tragically as did Meursault's

attempt to remain uncommitted and uninvolved in society. The tea which his sister Martha brings him, and which he takes for the welcome to the prodigal son, has been drugged in order that his mother and sister may more easily murder him and carry his body to the river.

The guilty as well as the innocent suffer from the world's absurdity. Martha's ambition in murdering all the travellers who came to her inn was to obtain enough money to escape to a country in the South, and live in 'that other country where summer crushes everything, where the winter rains drown the towns and where, at last, things are what they really are'. When Jan's wife Maria reveals to Martha what she has done, Martha cries out in revolt against the cruelty of the universe in which such frustration of love and desire is inevitable, and in the natural order of things. 'We have been robbed and cheated, I tell you. What use is our great cry towards the sea, the awakening of our souls? It is empty mockery. Your husband has his reply now, that dreadful house where we shall be all packed tight one against another.' The reply, which Jan has been seeking, is that exile and separation are the truth of a world in which no one is ever recognized. 'Understand that your suffering will never equal the injustice done to man,' Martha cries out before going to drown herself, rejoicing that Maria who had been happy should have to choose between 'the unfeeling happiness of the stones and the sticky bed where we are waiting for you'. In *Cross-Purpose*, there is no gleam of consolation, and the solution to the absurdity of the world suggested in the praise of the physical life in *Nuptials*, *The Myth of Sisyphus* and *The Outsider* is deliberately shown to be impossible. Here Camus seems to admit how personal the reply proposed to the absurd in *The Myth of Sisyphus* inevitably is. To those who are not born in a country of the sun there is no consolation. Happiness becomes a matter of luck, a question of geography or economic opportunity. In *Cross-Purpose* the absurd reveals an aspect absent from *The Myth of Sisyphus* and the demand for an escape from it is stronger.

The metaphysical pessimism which had formed the background to happiness in *The Myth of Sisyphus* is given a particularly forceful expression in *Cross-Purpose* by a crude but striking use of symbolism. Twice in the play characters call out for a reply to their questions. Alone in his room in the inn Jan seeks to escape from the haunting terror of absolute loneliness, 'the fear that there is no reply'. The only answer when he rings a bell is an old servant who appears and remains silent. At the end of the play this servant comes onto the stage again, in answer to Maria's passionate appeal to God to come to her help. 'Oh, my God!' she cries out, 'I cannot live in this desert! It is to You that I shall speak and I shall find my words. ... For it is unto You that I commit myself. Have pity upon me, O Lord, and turn your face towards me! Hear me O Lord, and stretch out your hand to me! Have pity for those who love and who are separated.' The old servant pronounces one word: 'Non'. In *The Myth of Sisyphus* this silence and indifference—which are the only characteristics of God throughout Camus's work—did not matter. Here, when the world in question is a profoundly unhappy one, they do. The expression which Camus gives to the absurd varies from optimism to pessimism in the degree to which his memory of North Africa is strong or weak. It is never absent, but it can never be a constant source of consolation when the problem of evil and suffering dominates.

The problem of suffering, of suffering in a world which has no meaning, is central to the play *Caligula*, first produced in 1945 but written in 1938. The action begins with Caligula's discovery of the truth of human existence—'a completely simple, completely clear truth, and a rather stupid one, but one which it is difficult to discover and heavy to bear. ... Men die and they are not happy.' The play is dominated by his attempt to find some way out of this closed world of death and misery into which the death of his sister—and mistress—Drusilla, has precipitated him. Caligula, whose liberty has neither political nor metaphysical limits, tries to transcend misery by the creation of 'a kingdom where the impossible is king'. His revolt aims at transforming the very nature of the world, at destroying everything, even the distinction between good and evil. The discovery of misery has given him an imperious need of the poetically impossible—'of the moon, or of immortality, of something which is perhaps mad, but which is not of this world'. His desire is that the destruction of all certainties around him will enable him to achieve this impossible ambition. His hope is that finally, 'when all is laid flat, the impossible finally realized on this earth, the moon between my two hands, then, perhaps, I shall be transformed and the world with me—then perhaps men will not die and will be happy.'

In his personal attempt to transform the world Caligula becomes also a kind of apostle of the absurd, a prophet determined to enforce recognition of his new gospel. He becomes, in the words of an English critic, 'the equivalent for Camus on the plane of metaphysics of what Undershaft is for Shaw on that of social ethics'. Caligula ensures that all shall be forced to recognize, through him, the absurdity of the world. He arbitrarily decrees famine and execution, rewards a slave guilty of theft with the gift of a fortune because he has remained silent under torture, lays down that the prize for civic virtue shall go to the citizen who has made the largest number of visits to the state brothels—attempts, as he says himself, to equal the gods in the sole medium in which human rivalry is possible, in that of cruelty. He is indeed for Camus what Undershaft was for Shaw —a figure who is horribly right because things as they are are horribly wrong. Throughout the play emphasis is laid upon the absolute logic of Caligula. Cherea, his enemy, recognizes it and admits that Caligula has a value in that the insecurity which he introduces into the world forces men to think. There is, in the world which Camus depicts in his early work, no reason why anyone should oppose Caligula. The world is absurd, and Caligula is merely stressing a forgotten truth. There is no logical reason to be drawn from the nature of things which says that Caligula is wrong and should be restrained. Logically the revolt of his subjects against him cannot be justified. They do rebel, however, led by Cherea, whose only reason for being with them is his instinctive need to defend happiness. Caligula dies with the cry, 'I am still alive'. The absurd, and the consciousness of misery which he had incarnated, are an eternal part of the human lot. He dies knowing that he has failed, that he has not transcended or destroyed the limitations of human existence, recognizing finally, 'I have not taken the road I should have taken, my liberty is not the right kind.' After *Caligula* the revolt against the nature of the world becomes, in Camus, a more modest attempt to improve rather than to destroy the nature of man's life.

Camus's intention in *Caligula* is the difficult one of making the audience sympathize with Caligula in spite of all the suffering which he causes. Like the Romantic hero, Caligula is unhappy because of his greater consciousness of reality. It is from this that he suffers and, again rather like the Romantic hero, 'sleeps only two hours every night and for the rest of the time, unable to rest, wanders through the galleries of his palace'. His absurd fantasies, he points out, cause fewer deaths than the smallest war undertaken by 'a reasonable tyrant'. The two most admirable characters in the play, the honest revolutionary Cherea and the young poet Scipio, understand and sympathize with him, Scipio to the point of not avenging himself for his father's death. Caligula has Camus's own love of life and horror of death. At a poetic contest he gives first prize to Scipio whose poem on death begins:

> 'Quest for happiness which purifies the heart,
> Sky where the sun streams down,
> Wild irreplaceable rejoicing, ecstasy without hope,'

and remarks that Scipio is 'very young to know the true meaning of death'. North Africa is present in *Caligula*, but present, as it was in *Cross-Purpose*, in a frustrating way. In both plays the existence of happiness intensifies the problem of misery and the hostile absurdity of the world. Caligula's rage and suffering, Martha's revolt and frustration, are, like Meursault's execution by an uncomprehending society, the darker side of the medal whose duality symbolized, in Camus's very first essays, the nature of the world. The absurd is not tragic because the desire for explanation conflicts with the irrationality of the world, but because the need and possibility of happiness are contradicted by the existence of misery. There are two equal and opposite certainties in the world to which Camus's early writings introduce us, but one factor is common to both. In neither the misery of *Cross-Purpose* and *Caligula* nor the happiness of *Nuptials* can man find any meaning or values. Caligula's suffering and Meursault's happiness exist in a world where actions—killing, making love, ruining an empire, drying one's hands on a towel—have all an equal importance, and in which there is no communion between one man and another. There is no such thing as crime, guilt, innocence, or action undertaken in common. The basic quality of the absurd world is that it reinforces man's solitude and renders all actions equally unimportant and insignificant. Having made of this absence of values the philosophical centre of his early work, Camus is henceforth concerned with the creation of new moral values to replace the lost humanist tradition. Now that he had stated the contemporary problem of *la non-garantie des valeurs*[1] in its acutest form he could move forward to some solution whose authenticity would be ensured by his initial refusal of the conventional and outworn humanist morality. His conversion to a new form of humanism provides an example of the artist who, having identified himself with the pessimism and negations of his time, lives out an exemplary destiny and shows that this pessimism exists only as a point of departure.

[1] See notes.

CHAPTER TWO

RESISTANCE AND REVOLT

absurd - a phase.

LATER in his career, an unwilling prisoner of his early reputation as a 'writer of the absurd', Camus constantly repeated that the absurd was for him only a phase in his development, a stage through which, like all his generation, he had necessarily to pass. Already in 1944 he was sufficiently detached from it to write, defending modern literature against the accusation of morbid pessimism which both communist and right-wing critics levelled against it: 'No, everything cannot be summed up in negation and absurdity. But we have first of all to pass through negation and absurdity because we have found them on our path, and because it is with them that our generation has to come to terms.' He had, reviewing Sartre's *Le Mur* in 1939, said that 'to describe the absurdity of life is not an end in itself, but only a beginning'. The problem was to find new values that would suit a time when formerly accepted sources of morality and truth were no longer regarded as valid, when rationalist humanism had no reply to the totalitarian menace, and the Christian tradition was still philosophically unacceptable. 'We need to know,' he wrote in 1944, 'if man, without the help of religion or of rationalist thought, can create his own values entirely by himself.' The need was acute for Camus personally, because he was already engaged in activities which the philosophy of the absurd could not possibly justify. He needed, both for his readers and for himself, to resolve the apparent contradiction between his ideas and his actions.

In claiming that the absurd had never been, for him, more than a literary subject which he had tried to treat without identifying himself completely with it, Camus could easily point to his early career and show that he had lived not as Meursault, Don Juan or Caligula, nor as an actor pursuing, through his different rôles, a multiplicity of experience. He had as a young man been concerned with the theatre and had founded in 1935, with a group of friends, the *Théâtre du Travail* in Algiers. In addition to adapting Malraux's *Le Temps du Mépris*, playing the rôle of Ivan in a stage version of *The Brothers Karamazov*—a significant choice in the light of his future development—he produced a play called *Révolte dans les Asturies*. This 'attempt at collective creation', which Camus did not officially claim as his own, since he wrote only about a quarter of the text, is a rather banal piece of social realism, enlivened only by some experiments in theatrical technique. It is based upon an actual incident in the general strike of October 1934 and is obviously written as a piece of propaganda in the class struggle. Camus was not using the theatre to cultivate his own self, but to improve the conditions of his fellow men. At the same time as he was writing for the *Théâtre du Travail* he was also working as a journalist in attempting to improve the living conditions of the Arabs in North Africa. In 1937 and 1938 he worked on the paper *Alger Républicain*, and in 1939 wrote a passionate condemnation of the living conditions of the Arabs in Kabylie. This he was to claim as proof of his fidelity to the cause of the Left when *L'Homme révolté* was in 1952 criticized for a tendency to provide arguments for the Right. In a quarrel with the communist journalist Pierre Hervé, conducted in the columns of *France-Observateur*, Camus offered to show him 'some hundreds of pages which prove that, for twenty years, when M. Hervé and his friends abandoned the colonial struggle for tactical reasons, I have never really waged any political struggle but this one'. The philosophical reasons for this political activity had not, however, been formulated by Camus at this time—'social justice needs no complicated philosophy in order to be carried out,' he wrote in 1944—and he was acting instinctively as he did when he joined the Resistance movement in 1941—'by the automatic reflex of humiliated honour'.

The statement of his need to convert these instinctively generous actions into a coherent philosophy is to be found in the *Lettres à un ami allemand* (*Letters to a German Friend*), first published in book form in 1945. In the fourth letter, the most important from this point of view, he describes how he and his German friend had shared the belief 'that this world has no final meaning', and had each drawn different conclusions from it. The German had assumed that this lack of reason could be used to justify all the excesses and ruthless conquests that would serve the only good which he recognized, the glory of his country.

'And,' says Camus, 'in truth, I who believed that I thought as you did, could see almost no argument with which to reply to you except a violent liking for justice which, in the last resort, seemed to me to be as little reasoned as the most sudden passion.' Such had apparently been his state of mind in 1939 and this letter, written in July 1944, does not show a great deal more progress towards the definition of a value which he can oppose to the cynical nihilism of his friend. He has not transformed his emotional feeling for justice into a firm philosophical principle, and is still in 1944 basing his demand for justice on the need which man has for it. 'I have chosen justice,' he writes, 'in order to remain faithful to the earth. I still think that the world has no final meaning. But I know that something in it has meaning, and that is man, because he is the only being to demand that he should have one.' A study of his semi-anonymous editorials in *Combat*, and of an essay *La Remarque sur la Révolte* (*A Note on Revolt*), published in 1945, will show how this instinctive feeling for justice leads to an argument which enables him philosophically to transcend the absurd.

The word 'revolt' occurs in Camus's early lyrical works and represents one of the central ideas in *The Myth of Sisyphus*. In the last essay in *Nuptials*, *Le Désert*, Camus describes how in the cloisters of the Santissima Annunziata in Florence he wandered in the rain among the tombs, reading the inscriptions to the dead. Night was falling and he sat at the foot of a pillar while the organ played in the church and the children leap-frogged among the tombs. 'Alone, with my back against the pillar, I was like someone seized by the throat, who shouts out his faith as if it were his dying words. Everything in me protested against such a resignation. "You must accept," said the tomb-stones. No, and I was right to rebel. I must follow this joy that goes (as one of the tombstones said), "indifferent and absorbed as a pilgrim upon the earth", must follow it step by step.' The tombs told him that his revolt was useless, that life rose and set with the sun, that he must acquiesce in the inevitability of death. Yet, he says, he cannot see what his revolt loses by its uselessness and he can feel what it gains from it. What he gains is the greater intensity of life of *The Myth of Sisyphus* where '*la révolte*' expresses the same individual refusal to acquiesce in the fact of inevitable death, to accept this scandal as being good. In *The Myth of Sisyphus* it is not only a question of refusing to accept death but of refusing to accept solutions which destroy the absurd. The absurd, he writes, dies only when one looks away, and must be maintained by the tension of refusal. One of the only coherent philosophical positions is thus '*la révolte*'. Camus defines it as a 'perpetual confrontation of man and of his own obscurity ... a demand for an impossible transcendence ... a perpetual consciousness by man of his own being'. 'It aspires to nothing,' he says, and is 'completely without hope'.

It is the refusal to accept which had characterized Sisyphus in the face of the gods and Meursault in the presence of the consolations of eternity of the prison chaplain. It is rebellion in a purely personal field, a refusal to acquiesce in that which seems, to the individual, unjust or incomprehensible, an attitude of defiance in the face of death which brings only a greater intensity to the sensation of being alive. The revolt, in this context, is a sterile notion which can do nothing but intensify personal experience—the whole aim of *The Myth of Sisyphus*—by a constant refusal of all solutions.

In 1942 Camus joined the group *Combat*, in whose newspaper he continued to write editorial and other articles after the liberation. In 1944 the word 'revolt' occurs in these articles, but with connotations different from those which it had had in *The Myth of Sisyphus*. On August 24th, 1944, in one of the first issues of the newspaper to come out in liberated Paris, he wrote that the reasons for which Frenchmen were fighting had 'the dimensions of hope and the depth of revolt'. This juxtaposition of two notions which were in *The Myth of Sisyphus* completely contradictory shows how the word is taking on a different meaning. On September 8th, in an article entitled '*Justice et Liberté*', Camus formulated what was for him the essential objection to Christianity and gave at the same time a further resonance to the word 'revolt'. Christianity is basically a doctrine of injustice, for it is founded upon the sacrifice of the innocent and the acceptance of this sacrifice. 'Justice, on the contrary,' he writes, 'and Paris has just experienced it in the nights lit up by the insurrection, justice is never found without revolt.' A further article published on September 19th distinguishes between the idea of revolt and that of revolution. The Resistance movement had, according to Camus, been inspired by the former and not the latter. Revolution was an intellectual idea, the passage from the instinctive movement of revolt to the realization of its ideals in history. It is distinguished from revolt which is 'the complete and obstinate refusal, initially almost blind, of an order which wanted to bring men to their knees ... Revolt is first of all in the heart'. This blind instinctive refusal is obviously the complete opposite of the lucid, personal revolt in *The Myth of Sisyphus*. It is unreasoned and emotional, originating in a primitive feeling of human solidarity and of human dignity. It was, for Camus, the equivalent of the unreasoned and instinctive generosity which had led him, as a young man still barely freed from his own poverty, to fight for the oppressed people of North Africa. It had brought him, at a later date, to play an active part in the Resistance movement. His early works—*Betwixt and Between*, *The Myth of Sisyphus*, *The Outsider*—had rationalized his own private revolt against the individual injustice of inevitable death. It was now his task to rationalize his protest against the collective injustices of war, plague, oppression and intolerance. *L'Homme révolté* (*The Rebel*) was to grow out of this revolt expressed in a series of newspaper articles in the same way as *The Myth of Sisyphus* had sprung from Camus's first essays. The starting point for *A Note on Revolt*, which Camus published in 1945, and reproduced with only a few changes in 1951, is a movement of blind, instinctive refusal.

It is a refusal which is peculiarly suited to the mid-twentieth century, with its original combination of slavery and bureaucracy. A *fonctionnaire*—a minor civil servant—suddenly decides, after a long period of servitude, to refuse to obey an order. This refusal, argues Camus, is based upon his instinctive perception of the limit beyond which his master has trespassed. His refusal to obey the authority which transgresses this limit is one which can be inspired not only by his own experiences but by those of other slaves. In other words, the rebel recognizes by his first movement of refusal the existence of an inviolable frontier which he will maintain for all men. His protest is an instinctive attempt to obtain certain minimal rights, and it gives birth to the basic truth that the individual is not a zero to be ignored nor a collection of impulses to be enslaved, but a unity which has an autonomous existence. The individual, by his movement of protest, affirms his own integrity as a basic value. In maintaining his initial refusal on behalf of others as well as of himself— Camus gives a striking contemporary illustration of how this is done—he affirms that this integrity is shared by others, both masters and slaves. 'We see already,' writes Camus on the very first page of *A Note on Revolt*, 'that the affirmation of revolt extends to something which transcends the individual, which takes him out of his supposed solitude, and which founds a value.' The world of Meursault and Caligula, in which no individual escaped from his solitude or acted with the idea of a positive value, is invaded by an idea which will make action possible.

In the movement of revolt the individual sacrifices himself for the sake of others. Camus had used the example of prisoners, in the Chinese revolution or the Siberian salt mines, committing suicide as a protest against ill-treatment in order to show, in *The Myth of Sisyphus*, that suicide can be caused by things other than the indifferent tone of voice in which a man may speak to his friend. In *A Note on Revolt* this suicide of protest becomes the very basis of human solidarity. Suicide for the sake of others constitutes a movement of revolt, as does Eckhart's preference of Hell with Christ to Heaven without him. 'It is in revolt that man goes beyond himself and discovers other people,' he writes, 'and, from this point of view, human solidarity is a philosophical certainty.' Coming back to the same idea at the end of the essay Camus finds that it can be taken as the basis for an affirmative reply to 'the only question which seems of any importance to-day: can man, alone, and without the help of God, create his own values?' Revolt provides a means of transcending the world of utter loneliness and frustration which certain aspects of the absurd revealed. 'There is something beyond anguish, and which is not a religious solution, and it is revolt.' Camus had defined this revolt as 'the most relative of experiences ... carried to the status of an absolute'.

This idea of relativity is an essential one in determining what kind of action revolt can justify. When revolt begins to act it can never aspire to the creation of an absolute in history in a revolution which is final and definite. The real value discovered in revolt is that of companionship and unity of interests among the slaves. This complicity can be maintained only by a faithfulness to the limited nature of human experience. The rebel must allow criticism and accept approximation. The only revolution which is 'adjusted to the measure of man' is to be found in 'the acceptance of relative aims and ambitions which means faithfulness to the human lot'. The attempt to attain the absolute is to sacrifice the individual to a false ambition. In all revolutions there comes a moment when justice and liberty enter into conflict and when the desire for absolute justice comes into conflict with the liberty of the individual. It is here that the limit established by the first movement of revolt must be respected, and where the rebel must accept the fact that, in human experience, no absolute can be achieved without denying this first principle of the inviolability of the human personality. Revolt provides both a discipline and an inspiration. It is both a call to action and an indication of how that action should be carried on. It provides a value which revolution must try to realize and which cannot, in any circumstances, be sacrificed to expediency. Were it possible to envisage a final revolution which would realize all ideals, in which the antinomy between justice and liberty did not exist, the ruthlessness of political realism might be justified. But since this is impossible, no absolute good can be held to justify the use of all means, and the very value which revolution is striving to achieve denies it the right to be ruthless. Revolution cannot use all and every means to achieve its ends. It originates in a revolt which was the affirmation of the integrity of the individual and of the existence of limits. Revolution cannot, without betraying revolt, cease to respect this integrity or deny these limits.

There are two dangers which threaten revolt and destroy human solidarity. The first is what Camus calls 'une prétension à l'éternel', the acceptance of a superhuman value which would cause men to be silent or to be nothing but 'the spokesman or echo of the divine voice', and the second the danger of political realism. Camus is far more concerned with the second—a fact which is natural in an age which has seen the replacement of religious by political persecution. Political realism justifies lying, which is a denial of the complicity created by revolt, and also justifies cruelty and the killing off of opponents. This complicity is not lost, 'that is never possible,' says Camus of his newly discovered absolute, but it is denied— 'and despair begins with the denial of the first truth brought by revolt, that man is not alone'. The rebel refuses the temptation of absolute Utopias which demand the sacrifice of his first value—the integrity of the individual—in order to be realized, and remains in his 'stubborn perseverance in the human being's limited status'. There is here a very close connection between the semi-political, semi-metaphysical thought of *A Note on Revolt* and the purely political thought which Camus expresses in his articles in *Combat*. He distinguishes between two forms of socialism—an indigenous French socialism, 'liberal, badly expressed, but essentially generous', which has its origins in the Resistance movement—and the orthodox Marxist socialism. The first does not believe in doctrines which are 'absolute and infallible', but in 'the obstinate, disorderly but inevitable improvement of the human lot'. It refuses the temptation of absolute Utopias which leads Marxism to progress to the perfect city through a succession of crimes. In politics, as in the metaphysics both of the absurd and of revolt, Camus's thought is characterized by an insistence on the limits of the human condition. In the same way as the whole argument of *The Myth of Sisyphus* confirmed the rejection of all non-human solutions, so revolt demands 'a human realm where all the replies are human', and, Camus adds as clarification in 1951, 'that is to say, expressed in rational terms'. The important difference between the attitude of the absurd and that of revolt lies in their fertility and in the realms of their application. The absurd is essentially an individual sensation. It is experienced by the individual conscience and its rules are applicable only to individual cases. Revolt, on the other hand, although at the very beginning an individualistic movement, can only really come to life by passing beyond the individual, and will inevitably be concerned with politics and political action.

In making this into the central theme of his constructive philosophical thought, Camus is being faithful to the original feeling of human solidarity which he had expressed in *Betwixt and Between*. In the same way that *The Myth of Sisyphus* was a rationalization of his instinctive knowledge that life was good and that the absence of all hope in a future existence intensified its value, *A Note on Revolt* justified Camus's originally unreasoned participation in the struggles of suffering humanity and the nature of that participation. Camus's philosophy always has its starting-point in emotion—'*la révolte, c'est d'abord le coeur*'—and he does not allow a contradiction between reason and emotion to subsist. In the development which his later work gives to the idea of revolt, it is Camus's emotional reaction towards the events and problems of his time which is the dominant factor. In the part of his work which he had devoted to the idea of the absurd, the first instinctive evidence was the value of his own existence. In revolt, it is with the lives of others that he is essentially concerned. What action can we take towards transforming the world in which our fellow men suffer and die, which will not at the same time increase death and suffering? This is the central problem of *La Peste* (*The Plague*), *Les Justes* (*The Just*), *L'Homme révolté* (*The Rebel*), and of almost all the political articles which Camus published after 1945. In what circumstances is action possible? Can this action ever take the form of killing another human being? Does this killing always destroy the complicity of revolt? How can we best reduce the suffering and injustice of the world? From being a description of man's fate in a world deprived of all values and significance, Camus's work becomes after 1945 a study and exploration, no longer of the nihilism of the absurd, but of the problems of action and of the service of humanity. Certain elements are constant in both periods of Camus's thought. Never does he accept any but human criteria or any value which could be placed higher than the individual. He is perpetually concerned with the rejection of philosophical ideas which would refuse the individual the final right of judgment, or deny his importance in favour of absolute values based upon either religion or upon a systematic and all-embracing philosophy of history. He never considers values as given in advance or as existing by virtue of certain eternal truths, but always as based upon and maintained by the original movement of human rebellion. He remains faithful to the physical delights of North Africa, finding in them a refuge against the complexities of a world of excessive abstraction. In both parts of his work he is a moralist. In the first in an analytical sense, as a writer describing certain human attitudes, situations and possibilities. In the second in a constructive sense, as a writer aiming at the creation of specific moral values which can be usefully applied to the problems of his time. From 1945 onwards he is sure of his first value. The revolt against injustice and cruelty which had come to a head under the German occupation creates the certainty that all such attempts to mutilate the human personality must be resisted. Camus's values are born under oppression and injustice and are essentially a protest against them. To a time which is acutely aware of injustice and oppression, his later work was to have the same appeal of immediate relevance which *The Outsider* and *The Myth of*

Sisyphus had had at a time when disbelief, hopelessness and the absence of values characterized the human lot. Camus's particular version of the philosophy of revolt, with its insistence upon moderation and the acceptance of limited aims, struck as original a note in the late 40's and early 50's as did his presentation of the absurd in 1942. At a time when the absurd was synonymous with gloom and misery, Camus had, without denying the gloom and misery, given it a new resonance as a source of possible happiness. When revolt was associated primarily with disorder and excess, Camus—more fundamentally this time—showed it to be in reality a demand for order and moderation. In the second case he was to be appreciated rather for his statement of the problem than for the solutions which he offered, for the way in which he conformed to the ideas of his time than for the way in which he departed from them.

CHAPTER THREE

THE PLAGUE

THE first discovery which the <u>rebel</u> makes, in his movement
towards human solidarity, is that <u>he shares a common suffering</u>
with all men. He is united with his fellows, but in a community
which more resembles a prison than a free and hospitable city.
He is no longer alone, but the hostile absurdity of his state has
not changed. The world is still absurd, as it was in *Caligula* and
Cross-Purpose, and the existence of moral values proclaimed in
A Note on Revolt does not open a period of optimistic humanism. 'In an absurd world,' he writes, 'the rebel still has one
certainty. It is the solidarity of men in the same adventure, the
fact that the grocer and he are both oppressed.' The only change
is that 'the evil which attacked an isolated man has become a
collective plague'. The absurdity of the world changes only in its
appearance when the rebel discovers his morality. But to the
new kind of absurdity which manifests itself in the plague,
revolt offers a possible reply. The world cannot be transformed
but it can be resisted.

This is the theme which runs through Camus's second novel
The Plague, published in 1947. An outbreak of plague occurs in
the town of Oran, on the Algerian coast. It is preceded by the
appearance of large numbers of rats which come out in their
thousands to die in the streets. The town authorities hesitate to
apply immediately the necessary prophylactic measures and to
impose the rigorous discipline essential to prevent the plague
from spreading. When the number of victims reaches thirty in a
day for the second time they decide to act. The state of siege is
declared and Oran segregated from the rest of the world.

It is from their isolation that the inhabitants of Oran suffer
most. The main character, Doctor Rieux, is himself separated
from his wife who left Oran some time before the outbreak of
the plague in order to pursue a course of treatment at a sanatorium outside the town. As a doctor, Rieux naturally occupies
an important place in the fight against the plague. Most of the
population, however, do their best to ignore its existence or to

forget about it and continue in their old life. They drink heavily, until the supply of alcohol is exhausted, and, although within a short time all the available films have been seen in all parts of the town, continue to go assiduously to the cinema. Various individuals react in different ways and are distinguished from the passive mass. Cottard, who at the beginning of the story had tried to hang himself, is pleased that the plague has come. It puts others in the same state of apprehension which had haunted him and allows him to escape for a time from the rather mysterious arrest which society is preparing for him. Rambert, a journalist who had come to the town to report on the living conditions of the Arabs, attempts to escape and to rejoin the woman he loves. He finally turns down the opportunity to escape when it is provided, and joins the fight against the plague. Tarrou, whose diary is used as a means of describing the town before and during the plague, organizes teams of volunteers in order to help Rieux to treat its victims. Towards the beginning of the book, after the plague has just broken out, Father Paneloux, a Jesuit priest, preaches a violent sermon in the cathedral on the theme that the plague has been sent by God as a just punishment to the inhabitants of Oran. Later in the book, after having been present at the death of a small boy, who dies of the plague, he preaches a second and less confident sermon. He recognizes the problem which the suffering of the innocent presents for the Christian, admits that reason is incapable of explaining the scandal, but denies that anyone has the courage completely to refuse all acceptance of God. We must accept or refuse everything, he says, for Christianity can include no half measures. He falls ill with a malady which, without quite being the plague, has many of its symptoms. Consistent with his own faith, he dies without accepting medical help.

Joseph Grand, a local government clerk, is at one point described as the true hero of the book. Unable, like Tarrou, to devote the whole of his time to fighting the plague, he helps in the evenings to keep a full statistical account of all the details of the plague's activity. For the rest of his time he is engaged in literary work—in the writing of a novel which never progresses beyond the first sentence, and which he can never bring to complete perfection. Grand is a less complex character than Tarrou, whose fight against this particular plague is only a continuation of his life-long struggle against plague in general, identified by him with the institution and principle of legal execution. Without believing in God Tarrou wishes to become a saint, to find inner peace in his 'morale de la compréhension'. This phrase is difficult to translate. Compréhension has both the idea of understanding and of comprehending in the sense of including everything. He dies in the last week of the plague, after Grand, who has also fallen ill, recovers.

It is never known whether the resistance to the plague and the organization to prevent it spreading are successful. After having held the town under its domination for nearly six months, its fury gradually diminishes. The serum begins to have an effect, the death rate decreases, and the town is eventually allowed to return to normal. Its inhabitants are reunited with those they love, from whom the plague had separated them. Only those whose loved one has died know the final separation, and such is the fate of Rieux whose wife has died in the sanatorium. Cottard, exposed again to his old fears of persecution, goes mad and shoots at the crowd from his window. He is captured and taken away. Rambert is reunited with his mistress. The book ends with the revelation that it is Rieux himself who is the author of this chronicle, written to testify to the violence and injustice imposed upon his town and to the fact that man shows, in times of tribulation, more things to admire than to despise. Rieux knows what the rejoicing crowd does not know, that the bacillus of the plague never dies and that the day will come again when, 'for the unhappiness and instruction of men, plague would once again wake up its rats and send them to die in the streets of a happy city'.

From one point of view the attitude adopted by Rieux and by the other characters towards the plague is exactly that advocated in A Note on Revolt. In simply doing his job well, Rieux is being faithful to the injunction always to serve man in a relative and limited way without aspiring to the eternal or the absolute. When Paneloux tells him that they are both together in working for the salvation of man, Rieux replies: 'Man's salvation is too big a word for me. I don't go as far as that. It is his health which concerns me, his health first of all.' Health is relative and attainable, salvation absolute and uncertain, and Camus's preference is given to the first. Yet it is not Rieux who is described as the true hero of the novel but Joseph Grand, who is engaged in activity as modest and unassuming as that which

Camus had admired as expressing the true nature of rebellion. Joseph Grand keeps the statistics of the plague. In *A Note on Revolt* it is stated that the action of the trade union secretary in keeping his accounts up to date is 'metaphysical revolt, just as much as the spectacular daring which sets Byron up against God'. True rebellion against injustice lies in the humble task which helps man in his fight against it. *The Plague* concentrates attention on the problem of suffering, and most particularly on the problem of the suffering of the innocent. It is, as Camus himself says, the most anti-Christian of all his books. Here again the novel expresses the philosophy of revolt since it is for its injustice that the rebel refuses to accept Christianity. Revolt is a demand for justice, and Christianity is 'first of all a philosophy of injustice'. It is the injustice of the death of the child which makes it impossible for Rieux to accept the Christian idea of an all-powerful and a good God. *The Plague* restates, in the context of the philosophy of revolt, the eternal problem of the contradiction between the existence of suffering and the existence of God. This philosophy makes no attempt to provide an absolute and metaphysical explanation but, faithful to its original impulse to serve man in the relative, offers only a provisional code of values. Since God allows evil to exist, says Rieux, it is better to give up all attempt to understand a problem beyond human comprehension and 'fight against death without lifting our eyes towards the Heavens where God stays silent'. The choice of plague, a physical disease of specifically non-human origin, to symbolize the hostility of the world and the problem of evil, allows the philosophy of revolt to be presented as a sufficient answer to the immediate situation. There is indeed no possible attitude to adopt towards the plague other than that which Camus describes, and the philosophy of revolt is peculiarly applicable to these particular circumstances. The book is not, however, to be fully explained solely in the terms of metaphysical revolt. The plague is a useful symbol for Camus—who warns the reader by a quotation from Defoe at the very beginning of the book that the imprisonment it imposes is an allegory—partly because it also has some of the same results as the absurd. Both Plague and Absurd cause the same evil of separation. In *Cross-Purpose* Maria had cried out, 'Take pity upon those who love and who are separated,' and once the gates of the city of Oran have been shut, separation from a loved one becomes, together with fear, 'the principal suffering of this long exile'.

Camus's insistence upon the sufferings of separation is one of the most surprising and original features of *The Plague*. It is far more fully treated and analyzed than the feeling of terror which one might have expected to predominate in the minds of the citizens of Oran. This insistence can be partly explained by reference to an article published in *Combat* on December 12th, 1944, in which Camus, describing the separation which had been imposed by the German occupation, wrote that for him separation is characteristic of the human condition. It is often the rule of the world, while 'reunion is only the exception, and happiness an accident which has lasted'. In imposing the separation of quarantine as a universal experience, the plague brings home to man, far more than another manifestation of physical evil such as cancer or earthquake would have done, the reality of the world. It is in the essence of things that those who love should be separated. This was something of which the inhabitants of Oran, confident humanists thinking only of themselves, 'sunk in stupid human confidence'—as Camus himself had been before death separated him from one of his closest friends—had ceased to be aware. The plague had made them recognize this truth. Caligula, who had proclaimed, 'I replace the plague,' had been accorded by Cherea the virtue of making men think—and had forced them to see things as they are. *The Plague*, by this insistence upon separation, is an allegory of the hostile nature of the absurd which had, in *Cross-Purpose*, imposed the same isolation. In both *The Plague* and *The Myth of Sisyphus* the absurd abolishes all belief in the future and all possibility of living elsewhere than in the immediate present. But in *The Myth of Sisyphus* the absurd was recognized by the consciousness, not imposed by the world's hostility, and led to the discovery of complete freedom. In *The Plague*, the liberty which it brings concerning everything but the present is described as '*affreuse*'. When the absurd assumes the form of the plague it holds man prisoner in the immediate present instead of liberating him. In this respect, the absurd is no longer a purely intellectual and individual experience, but a symbol of the universal fate of man in the twentieth century. Prisoners of the absurd, the inhabitants of Oran were 'this bewildered people of whom daily one section was heaped into the mouth of an oven and dissolved into greasy smoke, while the other, weighed down by the chains of impotence and fear, awaited its turn'. The evil which afflicted a solitary consciousness has indeed become, through the pressure of history, a 'collective plague'.

When *The Plague* was first published in 1947, the majority of French critics greeted it as an allegorical presentation, not only of *la condition humaine* in general, but also of the particular experience of the German occupation. The novel had been begun under the Occupation, and part of it—precisely that part which described the separation imposed by plague—had first appeared in 1943. The segregation of Oran from the rest of the world, necessary from the strictly medical point of view, symbolized the separation of France from the rest of the civilized world between 1940 and 1944. A modern city would not have been so unprepared medically for an outbreak of plague as Oran, and would certainly have hesitated less in taking the necessary measures against it. The Europe of the thirties, however, was in exactly the same state of blindness and unreadiness as Oran and the inhabitants of Britain and France, *'enfoncés dans la stupide confiance humaine'*. In any city—especially in Africa—cinemas would certainly be closed during a period of epidemic, but they were not closed in France between 1940 and 1944. It is unlikely that in a real plague a Christian, even of the most intolerant persuasion, would actually preach, 'Brethren, misfortune has come upon you: brethren, you have deserved it,' but French cathedrals in the first years of the Vichy régime were frequently witnesses to such sentiments. The impossibility for the citizens of Oran to protect themselves against arbitrary death which it pleased the plague to send them, differed little from the helplessness of the average French citizen in face of the imprisonment as a hostage or the deportation for forced labour which characterized the German occupation. Camus had written himself, in 1944, that 'this time is one of separation', and he gives, in *The Plague*, the full analysis of this experience. The *'équipes sanitaires'* which Tarrou organizes represent the small groups of men who originally constituted the Resistance movement, and it was in his own rebellion against the tyranny and brutality of the occupation that Camus confirmed the moral values which form so important a part of *The Plague*. Yet it would be an extremely limiting interpretation to see in *The Plague* only the description of a single historical experience. The struggle against plague and occupation are part of a wider struggle, not only against the physical evil inherent in the world, but also against the evil which men, by their blindness and indifference as well as by their cruelty, do to one another. Towards the end of the book, Tarrou's confession introduces this wider concept. It changes emphasis from death caused by disease to death codified and legalized by society. It gives wider associations to the word 'plague', and links the novel closely to the particular struggle which Camus himself was making against injustice. With it the novel becomes no longer simply an expression of the general nature of metaphysical revolt against cosmic, natural injustice, but also the statement of its central problem in human relationships. There comes a moment, in the movement of rebellion, when the rebel must face the question of his attitude towards those who might oppose him. Since he is protesting against suffering and death, has he any right to add to them by killing his enemies? It was this problem that had held Camus back and made him hesitate in the fight against fascism, until he was certain that he had right on his side. 'It has taken us all this time,' he wrote to his German friend, 'to discover whether we had the right to kill men, and to add to the atrocious suffering of the world.' It is a problem central to all Camus's thought, to which Tarrou's confession provides one, but not necessarily the only, answer.

The confession occurs one evening, after a day spent with Rieux fighting against the plague, in an hour which is, as Tarrou says, 'the hour of friendship'. Tarrou, unlike Rieux, a workman's son who had learned the truth of the world through poverty, was the son of a public prosecutor, who had wanted him to follow the same career. One day, in order to impress his son, Tarrou's father invited him to come and watch him in court. That day—he was seventeen—decided Tarrou's future. Only one memory remained in his mind, that of the figure of the criminal in the dock, a little red-haired man, who looked like an owl frightened by too strong a light, who bit the fingers of his right hand, who was alive and who was inevitably to be killed. Tarrou was filled with horror at this 'most abject of all murders'. Unable to bear life at home, where even the railway time-table, which it was his father's hobby to learn by heart, reminded him of this legalized murder, he went away and fought against the society which rested upon the institution of the death penalty.

'I did not want to be a carrier of the plague,' he says, and identifies it with the guilt which each member of society shares in capital punishment. But in his struggle against society, in his attempt to transform it, he came upon the same plague in a new form. The revolutionaries with whom he worked themselves pronounced sentence of death from time to time, and these sentences Tarrou accepted at first as necessary to bring about a better world, until one day he actually saw an execution by a firing-squad in Hungary. This experience revealed to him that, as he says, 'I had not ceased to be a carrier of the plague during all these long years when I had nevertheless believed with all my soul, that I was fighting against plague.' Faced with the central problem of revolt, Tarrou refuses to allow that the fight for a better world can ever justify 'this disgusting butchery', and limits his revolutionary activity to seeking to abolish the specific evil of capital punishment. Not, he tells Rieux, that he himself thinks he has attained a complete innocence where he is no longer responsible for the crimes which society commits. In this world, our smallest actions may bring about the death of a man, and none can claim absolute innocence. Understanding this, he has realized that all men are 'dans la peste' and he has lost all peace. For the time being, his action is limited to refusing to countenance any execution and to putting himself, under all circumstances, 'on the side of the victims ... to limit the destruction'. His more intimate and personal aim is to become 'a saint without God', to attain a peace of mind where he will no longer feel his guilt for the death of others and be a carrier of the plague.

Tarrou is one of the last people to die of the plague in the city of Oran. He is attended by Rieux, who can do nothing to help him but 'remain on the bank, empty-handed, his heart torn with anguish, once again helpless and without weapons against the disaster'. The plague, which had been for Tarrou only a symbol of the graver moral disease, carries him off as it carries off the innocent child and the fervent priest. By making Tarrou die of the physical disease, Camus is maintaining the plague as a manifestation of the hostility of the world as well as a symbol of the universal guilt of society. Tarrou's confession, however, gives a clearer indication of what Camus means by fighting against the plague. The novel is a didactic one, and all its readers cannot be doctors or members of Red Cross organizations. They can, nevertheless, Camus tells them, reduce the sum total of human suffering by refusing to admit arguments that justify killing under any form. Here the message of *The Plague* expresses the wider ideas behind the articles which Camus published in *Combat* in 1946. These articles—*Ni Victimes ni Bourreaux* (*Neither Victims nor Executioners*)—have as their theme the protest against the elevation of murder to the level of an instrument normally recognized and used to attain political ends. The twentieth century, he writes in 1946, is '*Le Siècle de la Peur*' ('The Century of Fear'), since it has seen the creation of 'a world where murder is made legal and where human life is considered as worthless'. This has happened, argues Camus, because the long tradition which accepted dialogues and approximations, discussions and reasonable arguments as means of arriving at satisfactory political solutions has given way to the domination of abstract ideologies. It is against the legalizing of murder— particularly through the divinization of history in Hegelian Marxism—that Camus's political activity, from 1946 onwards, is directed. Already in *A Note on Revolt* he points out how the basically moral exigencies of revolt cannot accept the moral nihilism implicit in political realism and the justification of ignoble means by supposedly perfect ends. In an article in 1946 he is more explicit and he writes: 'When one believes, like Hegel and the whole of modern philosophy, that man is made for history and not history for man, one cannot believe in dialogue. One believes in efficiency and in the will to power, that is, in silence and in lying. Ultimately, one believes in murder.' Tarrou's and Rieux's fight against the plague—the plague which is frequently described in the novel as '*l'abstraction*'—is Camus's own fight against the abstract logic of political ideologies, against totalitarianism in all its forms. Rieux's attitude corresponds to the 'modest political thought' which Camus is trying to formulate from 1946 onwards, and in political terms constitutes a plea for tolerance and liberalism. It is, in the opinion of Rieux and Tarrou, not because men are wicked that they are unhappy and cause such terrible increases in natural suffering, but because they are not sufficiently enlightened. In Rieux's opinion—and Rieux, as Camus says, is the narrator whose ideas dominate from the beginning to the end of the book—'good intentions can do as much damage as wickedness if they are not enlightened', and it is because men do not think that they increase their misfortune. For Tarrou, whose attitude is not necessarily Camus's own, 'all the misfortune of men comes from the fact that they do not use words clearly', and the source of evil is essentially the same. In addition to being a novel of 'medical humanism', an allegory of the absurd and of the German occupation, an attack on capital punishment and totalitarianism, *The Plague* is also a plea for liberalism. It contains, as its unifying theme, an apology for tolerance and for ordinary values, and a defence of happiness.

In 1948 Camus gave an interview in which he preferred Rieux's attitude as 'a human, strictly human possibility' to that of the attempt at sanctity of Tarrou. In the same interview he said of his own actions, 'Writers are on the side of life, against death and suffering. It is the only justification for their strange calling'. They are essentially, for Camus, the defenders of happiness. Throughout the whole of *The Plague* it is made clear that the place of heroism is 'just after, and never before, the generous demand for happiness'. If Rambert, the journalist, finally prefers to join Tarrou's volunteers rather than escape from Oran and join his mistress in Paris, it is not through any pressure which Rieux puts upon him. On the contrary, Rieux connives at his attempts at escape and will do nothing to prevent it, recognizing that Rambert has every right to devote the whole of his life to love, if he so wishes. No moral condemnation is made even of Cottard, who had used the opportunities of the plague to make money on the black market, and Camus merely remarks that he had 'an ignorant, that is, a lonely heart'. The unexplained feeling of guilt which had forced Cottard into attempted suicide at the beginning of the book prevented him from ever establishing any sort of human communion. He is alone because he cannot love, the worst fate, for Camus, that can befall a man. Grand, who represents more than any other character this apology for the normal which makes *The Plague* so different from the other '*romans de la condition humaine*' by Sartre and Malraux, had been at one time capable of love, and had been unhappy in it through no fault of his own. He was poor, and the love between him and his wife, Jeanne, had not been able to survive in an atmosphere of constant poverty. Grand always had difficulty in finding his words, and consequently never succeeded in writing a final letter of explanation to Jeanne, in asking for an increase in salary, or in making any progress with his novel. He is, by any worldly standard, an inefficient and unsatisfactory character, doomed to failure in everything he undertakes. It is in the portrait which he gives of Grand that Camus comes closest to the Duhamelian love of humanity for which he was to receive such scorn later in his career. Grand is Salavin transformed from an ineffectual near-hero into the actual hero of *The Plague*. In him, Camus's own love of ordinary humanity shows itself, as does his 'absurdist' predilection for the strange in some of the minor characters both of *The Plague* and of *The Outsider*.

There are four such characters in all. In *The Outsider*, Meursault's neighbour, Salamano, is an old man whose only real interest in life is his dog, an old and rather disgusting spaniel. He never shows any sign of affection for the dog. He is always beating and insulting it, but, when it is lost, he is extremely concerned over what may have happened to it, and terrified at the possibility that it may have been killed. The idea here is a rather banal one, and Salamano the least interesting of the four characters. The retired draper in *The Plague* represents a more interesting idea. He suffers from asthma, and throughout the novel Rieux always finds time to pay him a daily visit. The draper had retired from active life at the age of fifty and had taken to his bed. There he occupied his time in methodically transferring one potful of peas to another pot. He never, apparently, got bored, and found the arrangement highly satisfactory in that it removed all necessity to have a clock. At every second transference, he knew he needed a meal. The old draper is, in a way, an ironical continuation of the character of Meursault, or rather, of one aspect of his character, his lack of interest in the supposedly important things of life. In his prison cell, Meursault realizes that the simple act of being alive is so important that he could, if given the chance, live indefinitely in a tree-trunk if such were to be his fate. The old draper is doing something very close to this. He is Meursault such as Meursault would have been had not his bad luck and absolute honesty made his death inevitable. It is an ironical portrait, a corrective to the view of life expressed in *The Outsider*. Meursault was unfortunate not to have had the ability to keep himself alive, as did the draper whose monotonous action was certainly the best remedy for his asthma.

The two other strange characters are seen entirely from the outside and maintain an aura of curious mystery about them.

Tarrou's diary, which is, in its early stages, very much the journal of the connoisseur of the absurd, notes the description of an old man who attracted cats to come under his window in order that he might spit on them. When, during the plague, all cats and dogs were shot as possible carriers of disease, Tarrou remarks that in times of plague it is forbidden to spit on cats. No explanation is offered. The character, like the little lady in *The Outsider*, bears witness to the oddness of the world's absurdity. One day, when Meursault is lunching in his usual restaurant, a strange little lady comes and sits at his table. She feverishly takes off her coat, sits down, orders her meal in sharp, staccato accents, adds up the bill, lays the money to pay it, together with the exact tip, on the table, and then proceeds to tick off the radio programmes in her magazine. Meursault watches her for a while after she has left the restaurant, weaving her way precisely among the traffic until she disappears. She comes to watch Meursault at his trial, but gives him no sign of recognition. Her appearances simply add to the strange, unpredictable, almost Kafka-like universe in which *The Outsider* takes place. She, like the old man who spat on cats and the retired draper, represents the harmless absurdity of the world, while Meursault's condemnation and the coming of the plague show its more terrible and hostile side.

The publication of *The Plague* marks the third stage in Camus's progress from the nihilism of the absurd to the re-affirmation of normal humanist values. The first was constituted by the *Letters to a German Friend* with their sincere but still unjustifiable demand for meaning, and the second by *A Note on Revolt* which offered a set of arguments that could reasonably satisfy this demand. In *The Plague* Camus shows how his moral ideas will manifest themselves in a particular context and in face of a particular problem. In the next work, *L'État de Siège* (*State of Siege*), he returns to his North African and Mediterranean inspiration to illustrate the kind of happiness he is defending against abstraction. In *Les Justes* (*The Just*), he shows how the philosophy of revolt reacts in a different way to the problem of killing. Both plays continue his movement away from the absurdist position in which he had first made himself famous, and concentrate attention on the problems of revolt. Both lead up to and announce his longest work so far, *L'Homme révolté* (*The Rebel*).

CHAPTER FOUR

TWO PLAYS

ON October 27th, 1948, Jean-Louis Barrault produced Camus's fourth play, *L'État de Siège* (*State of Siege*), at the Théâtre Marigny. The *Avertissement* printed at the front of the published version informs the reader that although the subject is the same as that of *The Plague*, the play is by no means an adaptation of the novel. This warning applies on the plane of ideas as well as on that of aesthetics. From a theatrical point of view, Camus is trying to mingle 'all the different forms of dramatic expression, from the lyrical monologue to the collective theatre, through dumb show, straightforward dialogue, farce and the use of the chorus'. Nothing could form a stronger contrast to the deliberately monotonous narration of *The Plague*. On the plane of ideas, Camus selects some of the themes of his novel and gives them greater importance, just as he completely omits others and introduces new ideas not expressed in the novel. Most important in the play is the contrast between the regimentation imposed by the plague and the freedom inspired by the natural elements, in particular by the wind from the sea. Camus has returned to his first love as a refuge and source of strength against the deadening abstractions of his time, and as a final means of conquering them.

This theme is already announced in *The Plague* when, after Tarrou's confession, he and Rieux go down and bathe in the sea together. They find a temporary escape from the plague, and renew their strength for the fight against it. When the plague, at the beginning of *State of Siege*, imposes its domination over the Spanish town, the inhabitants know that when the wind blows again from the sea their liberation will come. In *State of Siege* the plague is far more obviously identified with totalitarianism than it is in *The Plague*. In the Paris production the character who represented it wore the uniform of a Nazi officer although Camus would have preferred a civil servant in a top hat. After the plague has taken over the government of the town—the authorities begin by refusing to recognize that anything is happening, and capitulate immediately when the plague reveals its power—it explains to the townspeople why it has come. Its aim is to replace 'the ridiculous anguish of happiness, the stupid faces of lovers, the selfish contemplation of the countryside and punishable irony' by an efficient organization. Now that order has been imposed, and the confusion of happiness and individuality banished, even death can be rationalized and made part of a system. 'You have your card index numbers,' says the plague to its subjects, 'you will no longer die by caprice. Destiny has grown wise, henceforth, and has installed itself in its offices. You will form part of statistics, and you will finally be of use to something.' The plague brings with it, as its gift to the inhabitants of Cadiz, 'silence, order and absolute justice'. The symbolism which remained ambiguous in the novel is here made explicit and obvious, and the attack against all forms of dictatorship deliberately made the centre of the play.

The plague recruits, in the place of the old authorities, the services of Nada, a drunken nihilist. It is he who is given the task of justifying, often in a highly ironic tone, the dictates of the plague to the townspeople. A mere buffoon if the play is read or seen by itself, Nada becomes a symbolic figure if the play is studied side by side with Camus's other philosophical writings. He represents the intellectual nihilism which, in the absence of all other values, justifies totalitarianism in order to satisfy its yearnings for destruction. 'Suppression, that is my gospel,' says Nada, 'but until now I had no good reasons to justify it. Now I have the reasons which the regulations provide.' For Camus, the absolute philosophies of history have been able to establish such a hold on European thought because they have based themselves upon its nihilism and despair. Camus's German friend had found in Nazism a reason for living and acting because no other was available. In the absence of other values to oppose to them, abstract ideologies, with their denial of life, have triumphed. This idea, central to the argument of *The Rebel*, is here expressed in the rather crude symbolism of the character of Nada.

The revolt of the inhabitants of Cadiz against the plague is led by Diego, who has to struggle between his love for Victoria and his duty towards his fellow-men. His revolt has not the quiet perseverance of Rieux and Tarrou, but more of the rhetorical protest of the Orestes in Sartre's *Les Mouches*. As soon as he rebels against the plague's secretary—a white-cuffed young lady symbolizing death—she realizes that she no longer has any power over him. 'As long as I can remember,' she says, 'it has always been enough for a man to overcome his fear for the machine to start to go wrong.' As soon as Diego takes consciousness of his power of revolt and achieves his freedom, the wind blows from the sea and the liberation of the town is at hand. Diego, like Sartre's Orestes, argues with the oppressor and in his argument expresses the author's own ideas. Like Sartre's Jupiter, Camus's plague has no power over the man who claims his own freedom. In the last scene of the play, the plague holds Diego's fiancée, Victoria, prisoner, and offers to exchange her life for the liberty of the town, or for Diego's own life. Diego refuses the exchange, rejecting the realist argument of the plague that 'one cannot be happy without consenting to the death of other people. It is the justice of this earth.' 'I was not born to consent to that justice,' he proclaims, and follows his refusal by a violent denunciation of the logic on which the political realism of the plague is based. 'I know the formula,' he says, this time completely the spokesman of Camus's own thought. 'We must kill to abolish murder, break laws to cure injustice. And this has been going on for centuries. For centuries the lords of your race have been infecting the world's wounds under the pretext of curing them, and still continue to boast about their remedy, since no one laughs at them to their face.' Diego's outburst is, like the whole of *The Plague*, a plea that ordinary people, with ordinary limited ambitions and qualities, should replace the hangmen of absolute justice. 'I hate only hangmen,' proclaim both Diego and Camus. Both plead that revolt should remain faithful to its origins, to the limit which it discovered as its first value and to the essential modesty which characterizes it.

Diego wins his argument with the plague, not because the plague recognizes that its attempt to impose absolute order and justice by using all and every means is wrong, but because death, which had been at the orders of the plague, grows tired of killing. She had been, in the past, sometimes welcomed as a reliever, sometimes merciful. Since she has been placed at the service of logic and reason, she says, 'I have ruined the skill of my once helpful hand.' Frustrated, deprived of his power by the revolt of death, the plague departs, and the wind blows again from the sea. Nada, as the plague goes away, throws himself into the sea, unable to bear the return of the justice which he hates. He is weary of everything, and cries out: ' I know too many things. Even scorn has had its day. Farewell, good people, you will one day learn that one cannot live well, knowing that man is nothing and that the face of God is terrible.' *State of Siege* is as much a refusal and criticism of nihilism as it is of totalitarianism.

It also contains, exaggerating a mere tendency of *The Plague* but continuing a central theme of *The Outsider*, an extremely biting satire against the hypocrisy of bourgeois morality. In *The Plague*, the judge Othon and his family form the subject of a satirical little portrait in Tarrou's diary, and, after the death of the judge's little boy, Tarrou feels sympathetic to his father but asks bitterly, 'Who can help a judge?' It is in keeping with the more violent tone of *State of Siege* that Victoria's father, who is a judge, should be a thorough hypocrite and should wish to betray Diego to the plague. It is his duty, he claims, to give Diego up, as he will then be acting in accordance with the law. But his wife revolts against him, pointing out that he had not the law on his side when he seduced a young girl who was attempting to obtain judgment against an unjust master, and claiming that, even if he has the law on his side, she has right on hers. The right she has is 'the right of those who love not to be separated, the right of the guilty to be pardoned, and the penitent to be honoured'. The normal human values of goodness and forgiveness are shown to be menaced not only by the excesses of revolutionary or fascist dictatorships, but also by the hypocrisy of outworn bourgeois morality. Such a direct attack on the hypocrisy which has perverted humanism in modern society is rare in Camus's work, for he is in general far more concerned with the criticism of revolution than of bourgeois society. For Camus, orthodox humanism as it is expressed in conventional middle-class morality is so definitely dead and discredited that it is no longer necessary to satirize or attack it. He does so only in *The Outsider* and in *State of Siege*. In *The Outsider* it is used principally for artistic purposes, to show the contrast between the absurd man and conventional society, and in *State of Siege* to liberate an instinctive hatred of judges which is only latent in *The Plague* but which is given full scope in *The Fall*. The morality expressed by the formal laws of society is at the greatest possible distance from the true object of his admiration, the beauty and freedom of the sea and nature. Throughout the play, the richness and diversity of the natural world form a contrast with the meanness of bourgeois morality and the terrible monotony of the totalitarian state.

The choice of Spain as the setting for *State of Siege* was, as Camus explained in a reply to a criticism of Gabriel Marcel, a conscious one. He is equally opposed to dictatorships of both Right and Left, and the ignoble rôle which the Church is made to play in *State of Siege*—very different from the rather sympathetic treatment given to Paneloux—is a deliberate attack upon the actions of the Church in Spain. The choice of Russia, in *The Just*, was dictated by the subject, the adaptation of the lives of the revolutionaries of 1905. These revolutionaries, Camus wrote in an article in *La Table Ronde* in 1948, had lived out 'the rebel's destiny in all its contradictions', and could provide, by their actions of 1905, the answer to any questions which the rebel of to-day might ask them. They, the '*meurtriers délicats*' (scrupulous assassins), as he called them, confronted the gravest problem of revolt: have we the right, by killing our opponents in a just cause, to add to the sum total of human suffering which we are trying to reduce? It is an eternal problem, but one which has an especial importance in view of Camus's own conception of revolt. For him, revolt is not a demand for absolute freedom or for the complete liberation of the individual from all constraint, but a protest against an excess of suffering and injustice. It has as its first concern the protection of the basic rights of the individual against violence. How can it, then, without denying its origins, be held to justify killing? In *The Plague* Tarrou had unconditionally refused the right to kill for any reason whatsoever. In *The Just* Camus proposes a different answer to the problem, and one which he will offer as a possible solution in *The Rebel*.

In the first act of *The Just*, the revolutionaries are waiting to learn the results of an attempt to assassinate the Grand Duke which Kaliayev, one of their number, has gone to make. Kaliayev, on his arrival, tells them that he did not throw the bomb because the Grand Duke's two children were in the carriage with him. Kaliayev, who had proclaimed that 'we are killing to build a world where no one will ever be killed', had

been unable to sacrifice innocent children to the hope of bringing about a better world. His failure to throw the bomb brings
him into conflict with Stepan, the revolutionary who, embittered
by his years of imprisonment, believes that all means which lead
to the triumph of the revolution are good. Stepan is prepared to
sacrifice the lives and happiness of the men who are living to-day
in return for the perfect happiness which the revolution will
achieve in the future. Kaliayev, on the contrary, loves 'those
who are living to-day on the same earth as I', and refuses, he
says, 'for a distant country of which I am not certain, to strike
my brothers in the face'. 'I will not add to living injustice for a
dead justice,' he says, preferring, as for Camus the true rebel
should, the immediate but limited justice which can be attained
in the present, to the absolute justice which can exist only in the
future. The scene between Dora, Kaliayev's mistress, Kaliayev
and Stepan, is, in its confrontation of the true rebel and the
absolute revolutionary, at the centre of the play. For Dora and
for Kaliayev there are, even in assassination and destruction,
limits which must be observed. Stepan recognizes no such limits
and maintains that they are incompatible with a belief in the
revolution. For those who are certain that the revolution will
destroy despotism and build 'a land of liberty that will finally
cover the whole world', the death of two children has simply no
importance. For him, 'we sometimes kill for nothing if we do
not kill enough', and the revolutionary must be prepared to will
the means at the same time as he wills the end. Dora foresees
with horror that a time will come when Stepan's ideas will
dominate, and men will come who, lacking Kaliayev's scruples,
'will use our example to justify killing and will not pay with their
life'. Kaliayev's solution to the problem of revolt, and the one
which Camus recognizes as the only valid one, is that the
assassin should pay with his own life for the life he has taken.
He will thus show, by his two actions, that murder is both
inevitable and impossible, and will illustrate the impossible
tension 'between the yes and the no' of revolt. There was no
question, Camus wrote in the programme note to The Just, to
which we in the mid-twentieth century could not find an answer
in the lives and examples of the scrupulous assassins. The choice
of Russia here provides an irony of which neither Camus nor his
audience can remain unconscious. It also makes the extreme
romanticism of the end of the play seem more acceptable.

Like *State of Siege*, *The Just* is a highly rhetorical and romantic play. Kaliayev, condemned to death, proclaims as he did in real life, 'death will be my supreme protest against a world made of tears and blood'. Death is for him the easiest solution to his problems. 'It is easy, so much more easy to die of one's contradictions than to live with them'—and both he and Dora are more than half in love with death. The play has as its epigraph a quotation from *Romeo and Juliet*, which sets the tone for the love between Kaliayev and Dora. They are haunted perpetually by the idea of death, torn between a longing for this solution to all their problems and the insistent appeal of life and happiness. 'I love beauty and happiness,' says Kaliayev, 'and it is for this reason that I hate despotism.' This conflict between their love of life and need for death separates them from the rest of the world. Like the Moses in Alfred de Vigny's poem, they can never know the warmth of normal human affection. 'We are not of this world, we are the just,' is Dora's cry. 'There is a warmth which is not for us. Ah, have pity on the just.' Theirs is the fate of separation from which the victims of the absurd also suffered, and in death Kaliayev knows that he will find the solution to this as well as to other problems. In his cell, after he has been condemned, the Grand Duchess comes to try to persuade him to repent and seek Christian forgiveness for his crime. Kaliayev refuses to accept the idea of his guilt, insisting that he has killed an idea and not a man. He has killed for love, he says, and will die for this same love of humanity. His death will be the final resolution of separation. 'Those who love to-day must die together if they wish to be reunited. Injustice separates, shame separates, suffering, the ill one does to others, living itself separates. Living is torture since being alive is separation.' This answer to Camus's eternal problem of separation—from which even the emotionless Meursault suffered—is one which is in keeping with the kind of character whom Camus is describing rather than with his own ideas. In *The Rebel*, which is more completely an expression of his own ideas, Camus turns from the romantic and nihilist Russia of the early twentieth century to a more sober and classical notion of moderation as a reply to the problems of revolt. *The Just* is, in all senses of the word, a dramatic presentation of the idea of '*mesure*' which characterizes true revolt. In *The Rebel* this idea of moderation is shown to be coexistent with happiness, and no longer, as it was in *The*

Just, in contradiction to it. '*La mesure*' had received other expressions besides the violently romantic one of *The Just* before it became the theme of *The Rebel*.

It is shown, in *L'Exhortation aux Médecins de la Peste* (*The Exhortation to the Doctors of the Plague*), to be the most reliable of the remedies against plague. The *Exhortation* did not appear in the novel itself, but was published separately, first in *Les Cahiers de la Pléiade* in 1947 and then in *Médecine de France* in 1949. Alongside ironic recommendations to doctors that in time of plague they should always wear sachets of herbs to save them from infection, and that they should dip their fingers in vinegar before feeling the patient's pulse, Camus included more serious philosophical advice. 'In a general way,' he wrote, 'observe that moderation which is the first enemy of the plague and the natural rule for man. Nemesis was not, as you were told in the Schools, the goddess of vengeance but that of moderation.' For the doctors of the plague, 'clarity of mind' is the best weapon. Inasmuch as the plague is a symbol of dictatorship or of the ruthlessness of imperialistic communism, or even of evil in general, the advice to the doctors shows that the real reply to it is 'moderation, sole mistress of plagues'. This moderation is characteristic both of the essence of revolt—'stubborn perseverance in the human being's limited status'—and of earliest Greek thought. In 1948 Camus's essay *L'Exil d'Hélène*, a preface to a collection *Permanence de la Grèce*, repeated the phrase that Nemesis was the goddess not of vengeance but of limits, and took the Greek idea of 'measure' as the basis of a criticism of contemporary European thought. 'At the dawn of Greek thought, Heraclitus already considered that justice set its bounds to the physical universe itself.' Greece had always been conscious of limits and respectful of beauty, whereas Europe, 'eager for the conquest of totality, is daughter of excess'. This condemnation of Europe becomes one of the main themes of *The Rebel*, which Camus describes as 'the history of European pride'. It begins apparently where *The Myth of Sisyphus* left off, but is far more than a continuation of the study of the problem of the absurd and of suicide. It is, in fact, Camus said, '*un effort pour comprendre mon temps*', a consideration of the outstanding problem of the twentieth century, the use of mass murder for political reasons. 'In a time of negation, it could be useful to question oneself on the problem of suicide. In a time of ideologies, one has to come to terms with murder.' *The Myth of Sisyphus* was concerned with a purely personal question, and the answer interested only the individual. In *The Rebel*, it is the fate of mankind which is at stake.

CHAPTER FIVE

TRUE REBELLION AND FALSE REBELS

IN spite of the universal importance of its theme, *The Rebel* is, for the ordinary reader, the most inaccessible of Camus's works. It is very long, and the detail of its argument includes, among other things, a discussion of Nietzsche, Stirner, Dostoievsky, Lautréamont, Rimbaud, the Marquis de Sade, Hegel, Proust, Bakunin, Marx, nihilism, communism, surrealism, and the French Revolution. Several of the sections into which it is divided were published separately before the book was produced as a whole, and a certain lack of continuity results from this. The book has far less unity than *The Myth of Sisyphus*, and there are fewer illustrations from ordinary experience to enable the non-philosophical reader to follow the argument. It was, in Camus's own words, 'a confidence ... the only kind of which I am capable', and it has the rambling and sometimes slightly irrelevant quality of a confession. Its real appeal is to the intellectual already acquainted with the thinkers it discusses and aware of the problems involved. Too frequently, the ordinary English reader feels like a stranger in the midst of a complicated family quarrel. Since he does not know the people concerned very well, it is difficult for him to judge the exact extent of their misdeeds. He can get the gist of *The Myth of Sisyphus* without having read Kierkegaard, Jaspers and Dostoievsky. His enjoyment and understanding are immensely increased if he has, but the book is so written as to be quite comprehensible if he has not. The same is not true of *The Rebel*. The fact that Camus finds it necessary to discuss the whole history of revolt from the Greeks to the present day tends to obscure the issue rather than to clarify it. The basic idea of the book is, however, a very simple one.

From *A Note on Revolt* onwards, Camus is sure of what revolt means for him. It protests against absurdity, suffering and injustice and creates a moral value based on the idea of moderation. Since it is founded on the protest of the slave against the infraction of limits, it is perpetually concerned with ensuring that a limit is respected. It implies the recognition of the integrity of the individual as the basic value, and the acceptance, in politics, of relative aims that will respect this integrity. If an aim is postulated as absolute, then this integrity is relegated to second place and revolt is betrayed. This is Camus's attitude, and one which he is concerned with propagating. Were it to be universally accepted, then politics would cease to be characterized by executions, massacres and concentration camps justified in the name of revolt. What Camus is doing in *The Rebel* is showing that any revolt which does not recognize that it should transcend nihilism and establish this limit is doomed to justify murder and lead to dictatorship. So far, in the twentieth century, it must be admitted, revolt and revolution have failed. They have set out with the highest ideals of liberty and justice, and have culminated in the police state. If revolt is to avoid doing this, then it must see where it has gone wrong. *The Rebel* is a diagnosis of the sickness of revolt, a sickness which comes from several sources. *nihilism means betrayal of revolt.*

First of all, it comes from a failure to go beyond nihilism. This is best illustrated by the example of Ivan Karamazov. Ivan protests against the world because it is full of unjustifiable and inexplicable suffering. He maintains at the same time that 'If God does not exist, then everything is permitted.' In other words, he is a rebel in his protest against suffering and injustice, but remains a nihilist in his ideas. Because of his nihilism, he betrays his revolt. Inspired by his teaching that 'If God does not exist, then everything is permitted,' his repulsive double, Smerdyakov, murders his father. Is Ivan to accept this crime which his own nihilism has brought about, and which it is incapable of condemning? The contradiction drives him mad. His revolt has failed because it remained basically nihilistic. It did not recognize that it existed primarily in the name of something, and that unless it recognized this value it was predestined to failure. The revolt of Nietzsche and of the Russian nihilists Bakunin and Netchaev had little of Ivan's protest against suffering but was deeply infected with the same nihilism. It was thus that Nietzsche's thought was perverted to justify National Socialism, while that of Netchaev led, as Dostoievsky pointed out, to a cult of murder for political ends. Since there are no values, then it is permissible to sacrifice everything to the

development of the Superman or to the coming of the revolution. It is basically its failure to escape from nihilism which has
caused revolt, in the twentieth century, to be so turned from its
generous origins. There are, nevertheless, other reasons for its
betrayal.

One of the most important is to be found in its purest form in
Sade, Lautréamont, Rimbaud and the surrealists, and lies in a
striving after the absolute. Sade demanded absolute liberty for
himself in order to satisfy his desires. In this he is unfaithful to
the teachings of true revolt which demands for each man only
so much liberty as is consistent with the liberty of his neighbour.
Because of this desire, Sade is led, in spite of his own generous
nature—revealed by his constant opposition to the death penalty—to the establishment, albeit in imagination only, of absolute dictatorships. In his elaborate formulation of his erotic day-
dreams he creates situations in which large numbers of people
are subject to the whim of a few all-powerful individuals. The
dictatorships which purely political rebels come to create are
foreshadowed in Sade's 'kingdoms of absolute necessity'. It is as
a result of this false idea of absolute liberty that rebels create
dictatorships. The poetry of Lautréamont and the life of
Rimbaud are also illustrations of this. Lautréamont is the author
of two books, of which the first, *Les Chants de Maldoror*, is a
long litany of revolt, and the second, *Les Poésies*, a manual of
conformity to established rules and traditions. This passage
from absolute revolt to absolute acceptance is, for Camus,
typical of the failure of revolt. The rebel who aspires after an
absolute excludes all limits from his first revolt. When he
wearies of the effort which this absolute revolt demands—and,
argues Camus, weary he inevitably will—he falls automatically
into the arms of conformity. Unable to bear liberty, he volun-
tarily enslaves himself. The fate of many revolutionary intellectuals is announced by Lautréamont. They too will go from
absolute revolt to complete conformity, from anarchistic
rebellion to communist discipline.

Rimbaud and surrealism reveal, though to a lesser extent, the
same characteristics. The true significance of the second half of
Rimbaud's life, where he abandons poetry for gun-running in
Abyssinia, lies in the illustration which it gives of this same
movement. Rimbaud gave revolt the purest poetic expression
which it had yet received. After that, he abandoned poetry com-

pletely and his letters from Harar show him obsessed exclusively
by thoughts of money. His initial refusal of all the commercial
and materialistic values of the nineteenth century is thus
followed by their complete acceptance. Surrealism, continuing
where Rimbaud left off, shared the same basic fault. Several of
the surrealists found their way so easily to communism
because, unable to obtain the best, 'they preferred the worst.
In this, they were nihilists. ... The true destruction of language
which surrealism desired with such obstinacy, is to be found not
in incoherence or in automatic writing. It is to be found in the
party line.' In art, as in politics and in philosophy, a desire for
the absolute is the ruin of revolt. This was something of which
Camus had been aware in 1945 when he wrote that 'the only
revolution which is adjusted to the measure of man is to be
found in the acceptance of relative aims and ambitions, which
means fidelity to the human lot'. In seeking to change life fundamentally, Rimbaud and surrealism were false rebels, and failing
to escape from the nihilism of our time, plunged into its absolute
conformity.

In the French Revolution, revolt was betrayed by too absolute
a reliance on formalistic virtue. Saint-Just and the Jacobins
killed, in the person of Louis XVI, the last representative of
God's law on earth. Their ambition was to replace this with the
perfect city of man. They failed because they did not take into
account the complexity of human nature, and tried instead to
make all men conform to a pre-existing model of virtue. They
were unable to understand the attitude of those who might
oppose them, deeming all critics automatically wicked. They
could not accept the approximations and the need for compromise which the truly modest rebel will recognize. Their
excess of virtue was as destructive of the individual as is the
complete lack of moral standards which characterizes nihilism.
They sacrificed man to a formalistic morality, while nihilism
sacrifices him to expediency. They were, in a way, the pre-
cursors of Hegelianism, which was to sacrifice him no less completely to the process of history.

It is with the advent of Hegelianism that revolt is, from a
philosophical point of view, turned from its origins. Hegelianism is nihilistic because it recognizes no other values but those
which will finally be produced by history. It destroys the formal
values of the French revolutionaries and of the bourgeois

thinkers who followed them, at the same time as it inherits and develops their destruction of divine values. It abolishes all values in order that the process of history may be more easily accomplished. Having dispensed with all other standards, it postulates the creation of an Absolute when the Idea realizes itself at the end of history. It doubly betrays revolt, both in maintaining nihilism and in setting up the Absolute as a final goal. It can thus justify the constant sacrifice of the individual in the name of an eventual good. Since it has been the dominating philosophy in the twentieth century, it is not surprising that this has witnessed an unprecedented disregard for the importance of the individual. Russian communism and Marxist totalitarianism, the constant justification of ignoble means by a noble end, and the systematic use of murder as a political weapon, all come, for Camus, from the influence of Hegel on Russian and European thought. The Hegelian dialectic is the philosophical basis of communism, and communism is therefore infected with its indifference to individual life. Hegel is the real villain of *The Rebel*. It is under his influence that Marxism ceases to be an empirical science and becomes a prophetic and intolerant religion. Communism developed, under the influence of Hegel, the idea that the workers' state was the realization of the Idea in history, and therefore that the workers' state was bound inevitably to come into being. Thus it systematically ignores any historical developments which might disprove its prophecy. Because Marxist communism is no longer a science but a religion, it persecutes those who do not conform, and finds its historical expression in the police state of the Soviet Union. In communism, Prometheus effects his final metamorphosis. He has abandoned all that first characterized him—his love of men and of justice, his hatred of the cruelty of divine and earthly rulers—and has become Caesar. 'The true, the eternal Prometheus has now taken on the face of one of Caesar's victims. The same cry, from the depths of ages, echoes in the Scythian desert.' The wheel has come full circle, and the rebel has become the tyrant.

The Rebel thus contains a criticism of some of the forms which revolt has taken up to the present day, and an explanation of their failure. It also considers the question why revolt should occupy so important a place in contemporary thought, and proposes a way by which man can escape from the impasse into which the betrayals of revolt have led him. The way of escape

consists of a return to the *mesure* which, in Greek thought, originally made the idea of absolute revolt impossible.

Camus points out that since revolt is necessarily against something or someone, it does not make its appearance as a metaphysical idea until a religious tradition teaches that one God is responsible for the whole of creation. In classical thought, it is only with Epicurus and Lucretius that the idea of the revolt of mortals against the Heavens comes to be expressed. Before them there was no rigid division between the gods on one side and unfortunate mortals on the other. Consequently, for the Greeks, 'the idea of innocence opposed to guilt, the vision of history reduced to the fight between good and evil, was foreign to them. In their universe, there were more mistakes than crimes, and the only final crime that of excess.' Having thus, in the early part of the book, announced his conclusions in advance, Camus develops this idea, determined to lose no opportunity to castigate the thought of the twentieth century. 'In the completely historical world which threatens to become our own,' he continues, 'there are no more mistakes, but only crimes, of which the first is moderation.' As in *L'Exil d'Hélène* (*Helen's Exile*), the Greek idea of moderation is used as a stick with which to beat the modern world.

It is with the idea of the God of the Old Testament that revolt such as we know it makes its first real appearance. He alone is responsible for the Creation, and the New Testament attempts to explain and justify this God to man. Christ justifies the existence of suffering by assuming himself the rôle of greatest pain. To all potential rebels Christianity replies that man must accept because Christ accepted before him. When, from the eighteenth century onwards, the divinity of Christ is seriously contested, he becomes 'just one more innocent victim, whom the representatives of the God of Abraham have sacrificed in a rather spectacular manner.' Christ no longer intercedes but seems instead, by the cruelty and pointlessness of his crucifixion, a greater proof of the cruelty of God. 'Thus the ground is prepared for the great attack against the hostile heavens.' The figure of God as moral ruler of the civilization against which the revolt is directed must be destroyed before the revolt can assume its full task of reorganizing civilization on the new basis of human justice. The failure of the revolt of Spartacus is an illustration of this. Spartacus, able if he so wished to capture and destroy

Rome, refrained at the last moment from doing so. His ambition did not extend to abolishing the city against whose injustices he rebelled for he had not the necessary metaphysical assurance and justification. He did not try to do so, and his revolt was mercilessly crushed. It is only when the French revolutionaries kill the king, the representative figure of God's law on earth, that revolt assumes its ambition to be a revolution. 1793 is the true beginning of the modern era, the beginning of the attempt to construct the city of man without, and against, God.

Revolt is so important in our own time because belief in a God whose existence justifies our civilization and our values has disappeared. With the disappearance of religious faith, the world becomes absurd. Camus's point of departure is in Dostoievsky's 'If God does not exist, then everything is permitted', and the Nietzschean realization that God is dead. The aim of Camus's revolt, like that of Dostoievsky's Christianity, is to show that this is not true, and that values do exist. Revolt may, in almost all its historical manifestations, deny these values, but they can never be quite destroyed. The true nature of art and the example of the Russian revolutionaries of 1905, whose story Camus had already told in *The Just*, guarantees their continued vitality.

A Note on Revolt had ended with the promise that the nature of man's revolt, the attempt to create order, unity and justice, could be elucidated in a study of the two main forms of revolt—political action and artistic creation. The aim of artistic creation was defined as 'an ideal work in which the creation would be corrected'. Neither Romanticism nor surrealism were true expressions of revolt in art. Romanticism had limited its revolt to vain ostentation, to the flaunting of the artist's wickedness and originality as a challenge to God. Surrealism never really went beyond nihilism. It is not in poetry, until now regarded as the apanage of revolt in literature, that true revolt is to be found, but in the novel. The ambition of the novelist is to take imperfect and unsatisfying reality and to transform it into a perfect, unified and satisfying whole. Camus quotes with approval the remark by Thibaudet on Balzac to the effect that *La Comédie humaine* is the imitation of God the Father, and the criticism of a Catholic writer that 'Art, whatever its aim, is always in sinful rivalry with God'. This is precisely what Camus now looks for in the novel—the creation of a man-made universe which will rival the world of God and, in its order and coher-

ence, compensate for the imperfections of God's creation. He finds the ideal novelist of revolt in Proust, who rescues his life from oblivion and gives it a lasting form in the perfect world of his own creation. Art, for Camus, corrects reality but does not deny it. To construct a perfect world in the abstract, excluding all reality from it, is for him, as for the Marxist critic, pure formalism. Reality must be transmuted and recreated but not denied. Order and unity must come from the artist's conflict with reality. 'The surest challenge which a work of this kind can present to the God-created world is to present itself as a whole, as a closed and unified world.' In Camus's aesthetic, revolt ceases to be an attempt to go beyond the disorder and incoherence of the universe—as it was with the surrealists—and becomes instead a source of order and harmony. In politics, likewise, revolt takes on qualities which are more traditionally associated with common-sense and with humanism.

In G. K. Chesterton's *The Man who was Thursday*, the hero, Syme, revolted from revolt into the refuge of normality. For him, the most poetical thing in the world was to hit the mark, to bring man-made order out of natural chaos. Revolt for its own sake was simply revolting—being sick. It is an attitude which Camus in part shares, though his reasons for doing so differ from Chesterton's. In politics as in art, he praises the normally accepted values of form, reason, tolerance and gradualness. He prefers non-political trade-unionism to revolutionary communism, Scandinavian socialism to Marxist revolution. Guidance for the rebel—has he the right, in his revolt, to kill those who oppose him?—he finds in the Russian revolutionaries of 1905. They consented to pay with their own life for the life which they took. In doing so, they proclaimed and maintained the limit which the first movement of revolt brought into being. Their example is one which will restore the value needed by European political thinkers and men of action. 'All can live again by the side of those who sacrificed themselves in 1905, but on condition that they understand that they correct one another, and that there is, under the sun, a limit which controls them all. Each tells the other that he is not God; this is the end of Romanticism.' *The Rebel* closes with this thought, with the hope that Europe has now outgrown its stage of nihilism and absolute revolt, and that it is now going to adopt an adult attitude.

What Camus does, in fact, in *The Rebel* is to judge the

thinkers whom he considers to be the most significant of his time from the point of view of a liberal humanism purged of its optimism and expressed in different terms. Transposed from the high plane of metaphysics on which the book is constructed, the *mesure* which Camus advocates can be rather crudely expressed in the anecdote about the Englishman and the nihilist. 'My liberty is absolute,' claimed the nihilist. 'There is no value at all to prevent me from punching you on the nose if I wish to do so.' 'Oh yes there is,' replied the Englishman. 'Your liberty ends where my nose begins.' As Kant expressed it in more philosophical terms: 'Every man should be treated as an end in himself and never as a means to an end.' Camus's revolt creates no philosophical principle which is not shared by liberal humanists. In fact, when he criticizes both Hegelianism and Christianity for sacrificing human nature and the individual to a supposedly higher good, he is going further back than liberal humanism and restating the Gospel truth that the Sabbath is made for man and not man for the Sabbath. Such conclusions were inevitable from the moment he argued, in *A Note on Revolt*, that the first refusal of the slave created the right of each man to be respected and treated as an individual. His originality lies in the way in which he comes to the same conclusions as the liberal humanist while setting out from absolutely different premises.

For traditional humanism, the world is not absurd, but basically rational. Man is at home in it, and the values which cause him to be respected as an individual are certain and absolute. In some way, the non-existence of God does not invalidate the normal rules of moral conduct. Camus does not go so far as the existentialist in denying that values exist, but insists that they can only have reality insofar as man discovers them by his own efforts. The death of God which, in company with Nietzsche, Malraux, Sartre and other thinkers of his time, he has experienced as the birth of the absurd, has thrown him back on the individual as the only possible source of new values. Setting out from a philosophical *tabula rasa*, he has recreated a humanism which starts out from the loss of faith which characterizes our time. He was impelled into doing so by the intellectual and historical atmosphere in which he came into consciousness. It is difficult for an ordinary English reader, protected by the lay morality still implicitly accepted in England, to understand the complete inability to justify moral values

which has characterized French thought in the twentieth
century. It is in the context of Malraux's *La Tentation de
l'Occident* and *La Condition Humaine*, of Nietzsche's *Beyond
Good and Evil*, Sartre's *La Nausée* and *L'Être et le Néant*, and,
most of all, of Dostoievsky's *The Brothers Karamazov* and *The
Possessed*, that *The Rebel* must be placed if it is to be understood. It is authors and books such as these, together with
Hegel and Marx, that dominate political and philosophical
thinking among contemporary Left-wing French intellectuals.
The premisses which all these intellectuals share—the rottenness
of bourgeois society and of the values on which it supposedly
rests, the absence of all divine or transcendent morality—were
automatically accepted by Camus in his first works, *The
Outsider* and *The Myth of Sisyphus*. He did not need to elaborate an attack upon bourgeois principles of morality or spend
any time proving the absurdity of the world. These were ideas
commonly accepted among French intellectuals, and Camus
simply had to make his own position clear. For the majority of
French critics writing on *The Myth of Sisyphus*, it was a most
acute diagnosis of the contemporary spiritual dilemma. For
Daniel-Rops it was 'the most profound testimony which has so
far been given of the "*mal du siècle*" '. For Jean-Jacques Rivière,
an 'illuminating analysis of the crisis in the modern mind, which
is a crisis of values', while for Albert Ollivier *The Outsider* and
The Myth of Sisyphus constituted 'the most faithful artistic
expression of the evil of modern times: absurdity'. It was from
this universally accepted standpoint of the absurd that Camus
set out to discover humanistic values. He never calls himself a
humanist. In *The Plague*, humanists are described as people who
think only of themselves, who are 'sunk in stupid human
confidence', unable to perceive the tragic nature of life around
them. In *The Rebel* Camus plays the contemporary French
intellectual game according to the rules. He does not come out
into the open and say that his criticism of Hegel, of Nietzsche, of
the Marquis de Sade and of the unscientific nature of contemporary Marxist thought is a criticism made by a liberal
humanist. It is one made by a faithful rebel. There are two
reasons for this, and the relative importance accorded to each of
them depends upon the degree of cynicism of the judge.

Camus may be, in *The Rebel*, simply playing the intellectual
game. Realizing that the very mention of the word 'humanist' is

sufficient to elicit the insult 'bourgeois' from any Left-wing French intellectual, he prefers to bring out humanist arguments under the name of revolt. Revolt is a highly fashionable word. Sade, it is agreed, is a rebel. So are Lautréamont, Rimbaud, the surrealists, Nietzsche, and, theoretically, the Hegelian Marxists. To judge them from the standpoint of humanism is automatically to put oneself off-side. To criticize them adequately, it is necessary to share at least some of their presuppositions. Otherwise, the criticism is immediately relegated to the limbo of bourgeois thought and does not apply. Camus condemns their nihilism and their indifference to individual human life and happiness from the point of view of the idea which they themselves profess: revolt. In doing so, he is taking them cleverly from the rear. This is the more cynical explanation of the choice of authors and events which Camus treats in *The Rebel*. Why, it might be asked, does he not talk about Gide, Freud, D. H. Lawrence, T. E. Lawrence, Malraux (an omission which Claude Mauriac was swift to notice), the English seventeenth century, the Encyclopaedic movement of the eighteenth century, the Commune of 1871, the assassination of Caesar and the consequent reinforcement of the Roman Empire, or the work of Bernanos, Ibsen, Shaw, Pirandello, George Orwell or Péguy? Partly, of course, because some of these are bourgeois thinkers, and do not, by contemporary French standards, merit discussion. But, more important, because their work has not been taken to form a kind of sacrosanct tradition of revolt and excess, in the name of which the most normal human values can be ignored. Camus is striving—*The Plague* is the clearest proof— to rehabilitate normal human values in the context of contemporary French intellectual fashion. For Camus, they need rehabilitation and he never says anything which implies his acceptance of the false humanism incarnated in the ruling classes of present-day French society. *The Rebel* plays the nihilists on their own ground and beats them at their own game. It is in fact the study and illustration of two paradoxes. The first, which it studies, is that the greatest rebel is tempted by the greatest conformity. The second, which it illustrates, is that revolt, which at first sight appears to be the rejection of all limits, is in fact a demand for a limit. In writing it Camus is turning revolt upside down. From one point of view, he provides us with a magnificent example of intellectual sleight-of-hand.

This is a cynical explanation, and it casts some doubt on Camus's sincerity, or, at least, on his intellectual perceptiveness. It makes *The Rebel* into an opportunistic piece of *littérature engagée*—albeit for the highest moral reasons. The second explanation of the choice of authors accepts that the book is exactly what Camus says it is—a confidence, and a confession, presumably of his own intellectual temptations. In the polemic which followed the publication of *The Rebel*, Camus wrote that he himself had lived through 'nihilism, contradiction, violence and the yearning for destruction'. That this is true is certainly the impression given by *The Outsider* and *Caligula*. But already in 1945 Camus put in a programme note that Caligula 'was wrong in that he did not love men'. *The Rebel* was composed, as Camus indicated by saying that it was a confidence that he had spent four years in formulating, between 1947 and 1951. Thus the confession was, to say the least, retrospective in nature, and composed at a time when Camus had already shown, in *The Plague* and in his other writings, just what was the nature of his own revolt. The revolt of Sade, of the surrealists, of Nietzsche and Bakunin had nothing at all to do with his demand for moderation. Revolt, in these writers, is far more concerned with the destruction of the limits which frustrate the absolute liberty of the individual. Hegelian Marxism had so long ago abandoned any notion of revolt except as a temporary tactic in the cold war that it would be difficult to say that Camus was tempted by it between 1947 and 1951. He did, it is true, speak approvingly of Saint-Just in 1944, only to show in an article published in 1946 that his approval was short-lived. If *The Rebel* was a confidence, then the temptations to which it referred must have been those which Camus experienced before 1945. The truth is, probably, that *The Rebel* is partly a confession of some of the intense likes of the early Camus—Rimbaud, Saint-Just, Nietzsche—and partly a repertory of the dislikes of his later period. Its point of departure is certainly sincere. The nihilism implicit in *The Myth of Sisyphus*, *The Outsider* and *Caligula* is the most convincing idea in Camus's work. It is more in its obsession with nihilism than in its treatment of the perversions of revolt that *The Rebel* is a study of Camus's own intellectual development. The question of his sincerity, however, is not one to which French critics devoted a great deal of attention. They were all far more concerned with discussing the probable effect which the book would have on French intellectual and political thinkers. *The Rebel* was universally treated not as an intellectual autobiography but as a '*livre engagé*' pleading for a particular attitude in the face of revolution and social injustice. Its critical reception was varied. The criticisms, however, bore on the question of the influence which it might have rather than on its merits as a work of literature.

Few French critics said it was too long, or did more than hint that its argument was a little confused and difficult to follow in places. None confessed to boredom. They were all interested and all appeared intimately acquainted with its theme. None pointed out that the basis of Camus's revolt—the refusal of the slave—was philosophically a little shaky, or that his conception of political activity—the murder of opponents—was not a very wide one. They were all so intimately acquainted with the idea of revolt that it did not occur to them to make a detailed examination of what Camus was in fact using as his basic weapon. They were more interested in what it might do and how it affected their own preconceived ideas as to the nature of revolt. Revolt was, for them, not a movement whose origins were to be minutely analyzed but something which existed in its own right. Few aspects of *The Rebel*, however, escaped some form of criticism. The almost unanimous approval with which *The Outsider* and *The Myth of Sisyphus* had been greeted changed to a varied chorus of assent and insult.

A clash between Sartre and Camus had been inevitable since *A Note on Revolt*. This was a condemnation of the idea that the end justifies the means, which Sartre was to express in a favourable light in the character of Hoederer in *Les Mains Sales*. In 1948, two years before Camus's *The Just* showed its author's preference for the idealist over the realist in politics, Sartre had extolled the political leader who was quite prepared to cheat and lie if by doing so he could achieve his ends. In spite of Sartre's analysis and praise of *The Outsider* in 1943, Albert Ollivier's enthusiastic review of *Caligula* in 1945, and Sartre's own recommendation of *The Plague* as the ideal novel of the future, *Les Temps Modernes* had been much less favourable towards *The Plague*. Two articles, one by Etiemble entitled *Peste ou Péché* and another by Jean Pouillon called *L'Optimisme de Camus*, contained serious reserves as to the value of the attitude advocated in *The Plague* and as to its accuracy as a description of the

Resistance movement. *The Plague* was, for Pouillon, 'the novel of the Resistance movement as people would have liked it to have been'—the fight of a minority against a purely external enemy. It avoided the whole question of the nature of evil which was the relationship of man to man. Instead, by representing evil as external and inevitable, it marked the end of Camus's revolutionary period. He had, according to the writers of *Les Temps Modernes*, forsaken revolution and its moral conflicts for the pleasures of a clear conscience. Etiemble pointed out that the action of simply fighting against a particular epidemic of plague was inadequate in modern times. In the next epidemic—which the Americans were busy preparing—Rieux and Tarrou would no longer be able to wash themselves temporarily free of the plague in the sea, since it would be contaminated with radio-activity. Creon, in Etiemble's view, was as necessary in our century as Antigone. He admired T. E. Lawrence for having had the virtue of thinking like Antigone but being able to act like Creon. Camus had not that courage. The ordinary morality of simply doing one's job was not, he pointed out, a sufficiently vigorous one for the needs of our time. After a real and recent plague had broken out in Egypt, a thorough reform of the medical services had taken place. No indication is given in *The Plague* that such a thing is going to happen in Oran or, symbolically, that it should have happened in post-war France. The political attitude implicit in *The Plague* was thus basically conservative, through timidity and abstention.

Replying, on Sartre's invitation, to Jeanson's criticism that in *The Rebel*, by ignoring historical reality and wishing to ignore history, he was serving the forces of reaction, Camus pointed out that his book implied not a refusal of history as such but of the doctrine which made History into an absolute. What he objected to was the divinisation of History by the Hegelian Marxists who used Hegel's ideas to justify complete political cynicism. The fact that Jeanson had not dealt with this idea—the central one of *The Rebel*—was for Camus proof of an intellectual duplicity which made him incapable of facing the facts of communist imperialism. The relationship, essential in Camus's mind, between communism and nihilism was not even touched upon by Jeanson. Sartre's reply was a variation upon Jeanson's argument that Camus had retired from the reality of politics into a haven of pure ideas. It was not a reply which Camus had expected, since he had replied to Jeanson on Sartre's express invitation and had, for that reason, addressed his letter to 'Monsieur le Directeur des *Temps Modernes*'. While Sartre used all his own particular gifts of personal analysis, irony and sarcasm, in addition to the existentialist arguments that no man can ever escape from his historical position and judge it object-ively—as Camus, he maintained, was trying to do—he, also, failed to answer Camus's main point. Camus had resumed the essential thesis of *The Rebel* in the rather portentous question: 'Does or does not *The Phenomenology of the Mind* authorize a theory of complete cynicism in political matters, and, for example, have there been left-wing Hegelians, and have they not influenced the development of communism in this direction in the twentieth century?' Camus, so Sartre hinted, had never in fact read either *The Phenomenology of the Mind* or *L'Être et le Néant*, and was thus unqualified to judge the moral implications of either of them. With considerable justification, both Sartre and Jeanson argued the inconceivability of so many men—the French worker of Billancourt, the Indonesian peasant, the North African rebel—working for communism mainly out of the desire for '*la divinisation de l'homme*' which Camus sees as its essence. Yet neither of them offered an alternative explanation as to why communism so systematically betrayed these men, and neither of them tried, by direct argument, to refute Camus's thesis. If, to the English reader, this polemic seems far removed from political reality, it is both because of Camus's obsession with Hegel and nihilism, and because of Sartre's refusal to come into the open and discuss the question seriously. The basic question which the two writers are debating—which, it must be admitted, only just manages to penetrate the smoke-screen of their language—is that of ends and means. It is a permanent problem, and one which is never very remote from any human society. It is both a merit of contemporary French literature that two of its leading figures should find it necessary to discuss this problem at length in public, and a defect of this literature that their discussion should be couched in such mandarinal language.

One of the minor points in this polemic was the question of the welcome given to *The Rebel* by the French right-wing press. For Sartre and Jeanson, this welcome was a proof that the book would, in the last resort, serve the interest of the middle class and of reaction rather than that of the working-class and of revolution. Camus pointed out that the traditional right— *Rivarol, Liberté de l'Esprit*—had not been at all favourably inclined towards *The Rebel*. Claude Mauriac had, indeed, been almost as damning as Jeanson, writing that Camus's book was 'philosophically a rather vain discourse, and politically all the more unconvincing as a solution because it had supposed the problem solved before it began'. Mauriac also pointed out that the final conclusion of the book was to justify murder, so that in fact it contradicted its own ends. What Camus did not mention in his letter to *Les Temps Modernes*—except in the veiled allusion to '*chroniqueurs bourgeois*'—were the enthusiastic reviews by respectable critics of the genuinely conventional and bourgeois right. André Billy, in the *Figaro*, had hinted at a coming conversion and a Christian influence on Camus. André Rousseaux had found *The Rebel* an excellent criticism of the revolutions of the twentieth century and written: 'the moment has perhaps come for the man of the twentieth century where anguish as to his destiny gives way before a consciousness of his real situation.' In *Hommes et Mondes*, the worthy parallel to the *Revue des Deux Mondes*, René Laloux was equally enthusiastic, and found it to be 'one of the most significant books of our time'. These reviews are strangely similar to the presentation of the English translation in 1953. 'With the publication of this book,' wrote Sir Herbert Read in his preface, 'a cloud which has oppressed the European mind for more than a century begins to lift. After an age of anxiety, despair and nihilism, it seems once again possible to hope—to have confidence again in man and in the future.' It was, in French writers, a similar tone of self-satisfied and comforted optimism which aroused Sartre's ire. The middle classes had been given yet another excuse not to do anything, and this excuse had come from a man whose early writings had been most successfully directed against the self-satisfaction of the bourgeois attitude of mind. What Sartre expected from revolt was a continued attack against the middle classes and their reactionary politics. What Camus sought in it was a cure for the excesses of revolutionary politics. It was thus inevitable that they should not agree.

There were other violent attacks against *The Rebel*, and the basic reason for them was likewise in the idea which other writers already had of the nature and function of revolt. Revolt is one of the key words of the surrealist movement. Revolt against God, against society, against rationalism and the intellect, against all attempts to impose the limitations of morality, tradition, culture and reason on the human personality, revolt against the very nature of things such as they exist and such as society accepts them. Surrealism finds its revolt most perfectly expressed in the poetry of Lautréamont and Rimbaud, in the attitude towards life of Jarry, in the systematic exaltation of his own desires in Sade, in the painting of Salvador Dali, in all efforts to escape from the tyranny of reason and of accepted custom and morality. It is, in its essence, an attempt to go beyond human existence and to free it from all limitations. Camus's revolt was a very different thing. By it, he sought to protect the individual against the absurd and the irrational, and to preserve something which he found infinitely valuable, human life as it naturally is. The real reason for the complete lack of sympathy between Camus and the surrealist movement, which led to the quarrel with André Breton, can be found in his first lyrical writings and their expression of his satisfaction with human life as it can be lived on a physical plane. Camus does not want radically to change the nature of human life but simply to protect it against violence and to improve the material and spiritual conditions under which it is lived. Emotionally, his own revolt has so little in common with that of Lautréamont and Rimbaud that it was inevitable for him to criticize them and find that they had, in his view, betrayed the true nature of revolt. For André Breton and the surrealist movement, they were gods placed so far above the intelligence of ordinary mortals that it was impious even to suggest a criticism of them. Camus, with his 'euclidean intelligence', had done so and had thus put himself beyond the pale.

Before *The Rebel* was published as a whole in November 1951, the extract *Lautréamont et la Banalité* appeared in *Les Cahiers du Sud*. This criticism of Lautréamont, and of the revolt expressed in his work, stimulated André Breton, the most faithful representative of the surrealist movement, to make a violent attack on Camus. The work of Lautréamont, he wrote, was 'that of the greatest genius of modern times', because it was one which systematically denied all rational explanation. In his criticism of it, Camus had put himself on the side of 'the worst kind of conservatism and conformity with accepted opinion'

and had tried to bring down to his own level something a thous-
and times greater than him. In the same way as the dispute with
Sartre had given him the opportunity to make his criticism of
Hegel and the Communist party more explicit, Camus used the
argument with Breton which followed from this attack to
clarify his other intentions in writing *The Rebel*. What he criticized in Lautréamont and the surrealist movement was a tendency which he recognized in his own character and which he
realized was responsible for much of the disorder and intellectual mystifications of his time—nihilism. Breton, he said, had
reason to regret certain of his early nihilist declarations in the
surrealist movement, because he must have realized, after 1933,
that they opened the way to Hitlerian barbarism. 'It was then
that we all understood,' he writes, 'that a certain nihilism which
we all more or less shared, left us defenceless against an enter-
prise which we detested with all our being.' It is this which he
attacks in surrealism, together with a taste for 'intellectual
annihilation' which he detects in it. He was not a conservative,
he said. 'If I saw anything worth keeping in our present society,
I should see no shame in being a conservative. Unfortunately,
there is nothing worth keeping.' Everything, he maintained,
must be periodically re-examined and criticized, including 'a
certain set version of revolt which is as different from true revolt
as night is from day'.

The argument with Breton was less serious intellectually and
less important than the disagreement with Sartre. The weekly
review *Arts*, where it took place, tended to specialize in literary
disputes based on the models so frequently to be found in the
early history of the surrealist movement, and the tone of personal insult which soon made itself felt on Breton's part showed
that it was less what Camus had said than what he had dared to
do which was important. Camus had suggested that ordinary
rules of literary criticism could be applied to the writers deified
by the surrealist movement, and that, ironically, it was '*la
révolte*' which put this criticism into practice. Camus's and
Breton's 'revolts' were bound to clash because both writers
were using the same word to describe entirely different things.
Breton demanded that he should have a monopoly of the word
révolte, and that it should mean exactly what he meant it to
mean, but if anything rather more than less. Camus had defined
revolt in quite a different way, but Breton paid attention only to

the consequences of Camus's revolt, not to its nature. He was not the only critic to do this.

One of the interesting aspects of the quarrel between Camus and Breton was the redefinition which Breton provided of the purest surrealist act. It had been—the definition had existed since 1922—to go down into the street with a revolver in one's hand and 'shoot at random into the crowd'. There was no doubt in his own mind, Breton pointed out to Camus, that the author of such an attempt would be lynched on the spot. 'It was a question—metaphysically speaking—of a deliberate attack against man, which was of a kind capable of reaching at one and the same time both the "I" and the "other".' [See notes.] A similar conception of revolt was shared by another leading French literary figure, Georges Bataille, director of the important monthly review, *Critique*. For him, the purest manifestation of revolt was the act of running amok of the Malayan natives. This is 'the movement by which man rises up against his own condition and against the whole of creation'. For Bataille, revolt is the demand for absolute *souveraineté* on the part of the individual, is essentially 'refusal to obey, uncontrolled and unsubdued passion', and can be found in the life and works of the Marquis de Sade and in the early plays of Camus. In Bataille's view Camus expresses revolt in its purest state in *Caligula* and in *Cross-Purpose*, where the desire to kill and the mystic awe implicit in the act of killing bring man to a closer communication with the sacred fury of the divine. It is curious to note how the whole of Bataille's long and sometimes very favourable review of *The Rebel* is coloured and confused by this obsession with *souveraineté*. The important thing for Bataille—as for several of Camus's critics—is not to judge the achievement of *The Rebel* but to express his own particular view of revolt.

The progressive Christian writers of the monthly *Esprit* are among the fairest critics of Camus's work. Camus has never hesitated to show his antipathy towards Christianity, both in his refusal of all idea of sin in his early essays, and in his insistence in *The Plague* on the unanswerable problem of the suffering of the innocent. His obvious moral fervour, however, and the sympathetic treatment which he gave Paneloux, distinguish him very sharply, in the Christian view, from Sartre, whose attacks against Christianity are of a much more violent nature. It is interesting to find, in the review which Bertrand d'Astorg gave of *The Plague* in 1947, that his criticism of it coincided almost exactly with that of Etiemble and Pouillon in *Les Temps Modernes*. D'Astorg admired Camus's moral integrity but noted the limitations of the attitude he recommended in *The Plague*. 'The best among them attack the effects: no one deals with the cause,' he wrote, and wondered whether it might not be better in some circumstances to prefer, to Tarrou's attempt at sanctity, 'the humility of a builder who is prepared to get his hands dirty'. It is in this article that the first comparison between Camus and Georges Duhamel is to be found. Camus's attitude in *The Plague*, d'Astorg observed, was very similar to that of Duhamel in *Civilisation* and *Paroles d'un Médecin* and one which is more suitable to a doctor than to a revolutionary. Albert Béguin's review of *The Rebel* in *Esprit* had likewise some similarity to the criticisms of Jeanson in *Les Temps Modernes*. 'Everything follows on too easily in Camus,' he wrote, 'in the cause and effect relationship of ideas inspiring events, and in the artificially supposed link between metaphysical revolt and historical upheavals.' This was not the only weakness, in his view, in *The Rebel*. He fully endorsed the criticism of 'a worship of history which is in fact one of the monsters whose greed is devouring us', but had more serious doubts on the value of Camus's revolt as a source of morality. It was based, he recognized, on the demand for happiness. This, for a Christian, was not enough. It was the demand for salvation and for salvation only, which could be opposed as a genuine value to 'the imperious movement of History'. Even the most favourable reviews did not refrain from pointing out how their revolt was superior to Camus's. The communist press, when it eventually found time to criticize *The Rebel*, attacked it with violence and insinuated that Camus had been paid in dollars to write it. The idea of the State Department subsidising such esoteric moves in the anti-communist game is funny to the English but not, apparently, to the French.

The varied reception which *The Rebel* was given by literary critics had thus been foreshadowed by the articles written on *The Plague* in 1947 and 1948. This was Camus's first major work which contained a positive moral message, and, in spite of its immense popularity with the general public—100,000 copies were sold within six months of its publication—the morality did not receive universal approval. Artistically, it was greeted as a masterpiece—indeed the only works by Camus to have been unfavourably received on artistic grounds were *State of Siege* and *The Just*—and its perfect use of transition, allegory and symbol was much admired. For ordinary people it satisfied the yearning for the normal, the humanly acceptable, the sensible and the practical after an epoch of excess and murderous fanaticism. Camus struck a note of optimism in man and in human nature, of faith in a purely practical and empirical code of values that came like a breath of fresh air after the pessimism of Sartre, Kafka, Faulkner, Gary and other writers whose popularity expressed the post-war state of mind in France. Literary critics, however, have as their task the deeper analysis of an author's meaning and intentions, and it was in this deeper analysis that some of the limitations of Camus's attitude became apparent. Gaeton Picon pointed out that the morality of simply not being oneself a carrier of infection was an inadequate one in the tragic atmosphere of our time. The attitude of non-intervention—which was what the morality of *The Plague* amounted to— was 'the morality of the men of the nineteenth century who have allowed the catastrophe to happen'. The criticism of Pouillon, Etiemble and of Bertrand d'Astorg—who described *The Plague* as 'a new humanitarianism'—has already been quoted. While many critics, both of right and left, were extremely enthusiastic—Marcel Thiébaut admired Camus for reintegrating into an absurd world the moral principles which govern a world which is not absurd, Roger Stéphane in the socialist *La Revue Internationale* described him as 'the most faithful painter of daily life under the occupation' and *The Plague* as the worthy continuation of Malraux's *L'Espoir*— most of them chose to make serious reservations as to the implications of the attitude described in *The Plague*. In *La Nef* J. J. Rivieri described it as 'a leap in the dark' and, in the same review, Jacques Sorel, writing on the translation of Richard Wright's *Native Son*, found that *The Plague* was 'almost indecent compared to such a book'. When the positive content of the moral message of *The Plague* is analyzed it does, it is true, amount very much to a plea for the International Red Cross. That this was partly Camus's deliberate intention is revealed in his open letter to Sartre in 1952, and it was no accident that a young doctor found Bernard Rieux to be the best representative, in fiction, of '*un humanisme médical contemporain*'. As long as the book remains on the plane of a simple description of an epidemic of plague this attitude is entirely satisfactory. It is when the particular allegory of the book demands that its moral message should also be considered in relation to the German occupation and the Resistance movement that it shows its insufficiencies. Camus's basic refusal to accept that men are responsible for the evil which they cause, and that they must be resisted, if necessary by violence, detracts from the value of *The Plague* as a source of morality. The identification of the very personal existence and ambitions of the German nation with the quite impersonal character of the microbes of the plague by-passes this problem. Camus's dilemma is here that of the traditional liberal humanist. If man is good—as the liberal humanist believes him to be —and if all men are brothers—as Camus's revolt shows them to be—then how is it that men are wicked and how can evil be resisted at the same time as metaphysical solidarity is maintained? At what point does a man so menace his fellows that metaphysical solidarity must be sacrificed to safety? Camus does not honestly confront this problem. For him, man is good and all evil comes either from outside man or from the fact that he is misled by wrong ideas. The note of resignation on which *The Plague* closes is a direct result of this belief that, basically, man is not responsible. If he were responsible, then action could be taken both to find the guilty—those who sent the plague and those who allowed it to arrive—and to prevent the same thing from happening again. The acceptance that evil will return, implied in the ending of *The Plague*, is an abdication of the ideal, '*De la Résistance à la Révolution*', which had been the inspiration of *Combat*. From *The Plague* onwards Camus's thought does take on a less revolutionary aspect. This is because, in response to the dangers and challenges of political events in the middle and late forties, Camus had become increasingly conscious of the menace which Russian imperialistic communism constituted for the freedom and the integrity of the individual. Like George Orwell and Arthur Koestler—indeed, like any honest left-wing thinker in mid-twentieth-century Europe—Camus is diverted from the criticism of the abuses of capitalist society by the need to attack the greater menace of totalitarian communism. He gives up the ideal of '*de la résistance à la révolution*' exactly to the extent that the revolution which threatens to become dominant is a complete contradiction of the original ideas of revolt. It is not Camus's revolt which changes between 1945 and 1951, but the source of the dangers which threaten the individual. There is little evolution in his thought between 1945 and 1951. The real change in his concept of revolt had taken place between the publication of *The Myth of Sisyphus* and that of *A Note on Revolt*.

It is important to remember this when one is tempted to equate the violence of Meursault's and Caligula's revolt against society and the world with Camus's activity in the Resistance movement. These characters represent his first, early, adolescent revolt—lyrical, personal and extreme— against the world and its absurdity. When he was in the Resistance movement, Camus was inspired not by these ideas but by those which he was to express in *The Plague* and *The Rebel*. He passes from a violent, personal and intolerant revolt in his early work to a revolt which seeks essentially moderation, tolerance and communion with other men. Certain elements—the love of physical life, the hatred of hypocrisy and the refusal of non-human criteria—are, of course, common to both periods. The fact that *The Rebel* and *The Plague* are less satisfying respectively as works of art than *The Myth of Sisyphus* and *The Outsider* is due mainly to the fact that Camus is cramping his intensely individualistic and passionate temperament to express ideas with which he feels less purely emotional sympathy. His relative failure in this part of his work—which, after *La Chute* and *L'Exil et le Royaume*, future critics may call his middle, deliberately humanistic period— shows the extreme difficulty of what he is trying to do: to express, as a modern writer, the ideals of liberal humanism.

In the closing pages of *The Liberal Imagination*, Lionel Trilling points out that there exists a lack of sympathy between the 'tradition of democratic liberalism as we know it' and the most significant of the modern European writers. 'Yeats and Eliot,' he writes, 'Proust and Joyce, Lawrence and Gide— these men do not seem to confirm us in the social and political ideas which we hold.' Trilling could have added to his list the names of Malraux, Sartre, Kafka, Graham Greene, Aldous Huxley, Evelyn Waugh, André Breton, and the host of poets stemming from the tradition of Baudelaire, Rimbaud and

Mallarmé. While the early Camus of *The Outsider* and *The Myth of Sisyphus* illustrates the dichotomy of which Lionel Trilling speaks, the later Camus of *The Plague* and *The Rebel* seems almost like an effort to refute him. In criticizing the tradition of revolt such as it has existed in part up to the present day, Camus seems to bring a certain current of opinion back into the main stream of liberal thought. In insisting upon the value of the individual, on the value of empiricism and modesty in politics, on the need for moderation and comprehension, Camus is restating the basic principles of liberal democracy. The extent to which he manages convincingly to bridge the gap between liberal democratic society and the climate of opinion predominant in the literature of this society is the true criterion of his activity as '*l'écrivain de la révolte*'. His achievement cannot be judged by comparison with that of any other contemporary writer for he has been alone, so far, in attempting it.

CHAPTER SIX

THE CREATIVE REVIVAL

BETWEEN 1951 and 1956 Camus published no major work. He limited his activity to clarifying the intentions of his work so far, to collecting political and polemical texts in the second volume of *Actuelles* and lyrical texts in *L'Été*, and to writing occasional prefaces. One of these was an introduction to a new translation of *The Ballad of Reading Gaol*, and is interesting in that it shows the survival of the Wilde legend in French literature. More important is a preface to the complete works of Roger Martin du Gard which served as an introduction to their publication in 1955 in the *Bibliothèque de la Pléiade*. This preface is one of the most sympathetic which Camus has written or Roger Martin du Gard received. It confirms the complete reversal of attitude which Camus has effected since 1942, by marking a preference for Antoine over Jacques Thibault, and for Tolstoy over Dostoievsky. It shows how Camus has come to regard literature, not so much as a means of protesting against life, but of proceeding towards a deeper understanding of it. His study of Martin du Gard seems now to be bearing fruit in the novel *La Chute* and in the short stories of *L'Exil et le Royaume*, in the same way as his earlier reading of Kafka and Kierkegaard bore fruit in *The Outsider* and *The Myth of Sisyphus*. Camus's return to creative and imaginative writing is a most welcome one, especially as *The Rebel*—like Sartre's study of Jean Genet and Malraux's art criticism—seemed to mark a stage beyond which it was difficult to make any further progress in the same direction.

It is one of the points of resemblance between Sartre, Malraux and Camus that they should all three have established their reputation by writing metaphysical novels before choosing to express their metaphysics in a different medium. From the point of view of the general interest of their works, the progress from *La Condition Humaine* (*Man's Fate*) to *Les Voix du Silence* (*The Voices of Silence*), and the apparent abandonment of *Les Chemins de la Liberté* (*Roads to Freedom*) are regrettable. Although the quality of the thought may be finer in the later, more philosophical works, and the resolution of the writer's problems appear closer, works such as Sartre's *Saint-Genet, Comédien et Martyr* represent, from a literary standpoint, a decrease in interest if not in merit. It was particularly regrettable in Camus's own case, for his two novels, *The Outsider* and *The Plague*, undoubtedly contain some of his best writing, and are the most convincing expressions not only of his absurdist philosophy, but also of his new humanism. *La Chute* (*The Fall*) and the short stories of *L'Exil et le Royaume* (*Exile and the Kingdom*) mark a return to creative writing after a silence during which some of his warmest admirers had begun to wonder whether he had exhausted all he had to say.

The Fall was first published in Paris in May 1956, and it is the most ambiguous work which Camus has as yet published. Although *The Plague* and *The Outsider* might be read on different planes, and do in fact yield many different meanings on analysis, their general significance is quite clear. This is not the case with *The Fall*, and critical reception in both France and England has reflected the disquiet and uncertainty which the novel produces in the mind of the reader. In *The Outsider*, Meursault clearly has the sympathy of the author, all events are presented as he sees them, and from his point of view, and the autobiographical elements are strong enough for us to identify him with one of Camus's own moods. In *The Plague*, Camus has stated quite clearly that Rieux is the Narrator and that it is his point of view which predominates, while at the same time it is clear that Tarrou has much of the author's sympathy, and that Camus is fond of all his characters. In *The Fall*, it is only possible to identify the central character Jean-Baptiste Clamence with Camus himself if we discount almost everything else which he has written. In his most pessimistic vision of the absurd—in *Caligula* and *Cross-Purpose*—Camus remained a humanist and a defender of man against the absurdity of the world. In *The Outsider*, *The Plague* and *The Rebel*, he insisted upon the innocence of man and the natural injustice of the world, and upon the fact that man caused evil and suffering only when he was misled by false ideas. In *The Fall*, all this seems to have been changed. The narrator knows himself to be self-centred, dishonest, cowardly, hypocritical and vain, and has assumed the task of proving to all other men that they are no different from him. His judgments upon mankind are of unrelieved pessimism. 'A single sentence will suffice for modern man;' he says, 'he fornicated and read the papers.' When he speaks of the subjects which have obsessed Camus himself—physical torture, the massacre of the Jews, the legalisation of murder, the ruthlessness of politicians and the intolerance of intellectuals—he does so with a gloating satisfaction. He even uses, to support his cynicism about mankind, an incident already mentioned in *The Rebel*, of the Nazi officer who forced a Greek mother to choose which one of her sons was to be executed as a hostage. His intention, however, is quite the opposite of that of *The Rebel*. In *The Fall*, such acts of criminality are used not as arguments against man's intolerance and fanaticism, but as excuses for despising and hating him. Clamence seems to think that, if man suffers, then it is entirely his own fault.

The Fall is a book of absolute pessimism, and the temptation to identify Clamence with Camus and thus see his pessimism as Camus's own attitude is considerable. When the narrator speaks of the ease which he had in living, of the neatness with which all his intentions were realized, of the charm which radiated from him, one is irresistibly reminded of Camus himself. All those who have written of him as a person agree on Camus's charm of manner and agreeable character. When Jean-Baptiste Clamence describes the delight with which he espoused the cause of the widow and the orphan, his sincere defence of the innocent against the ruthless mechanism of the law, his daily putting into practice of the best humanist ideas, it seems quite an obvious transposition of the noble rôle which Camus has always played in politics and journalism. Some of the more frivolous remarks which Clamence makes in his general accusation against mankind are also highly reminiscent of Camus's own preoccupations. He speaks of a prostitute who had written her memoirs for 'a confessional paper quite open to modern ideas'—an obvious hit at Sartre's *Les Temps Modernes* which once published such a life story. There is the almost inevitable little dig at communist intellectuals in the description of a man talking 'with the certainty and assurance of an intellectual announcing the classless society'. Camus's permanent obsession with suicide finds its expression in the narrator's monologue, as does his satirical awareness of the precision and grammatical perfection of his own prose and of his use of the imperfect of the subjunctive. In fact, the resemblances between narrator and author are so considerable as to have caused certain critics to identify them completely with each other.

If one does so, there is only one possible conclusion: Camus is giving up his humanistic attitude and is going towards the Catholic Church. The narrator's name seems to provide a strong hint that this may be the case. Donat O'Donnell has pointed out that it is an obvious adaptation of John the Baptist—Jean-Baptiste—crying in the wilderness: '*vox clamans in deserto*'. It is possible that the novel expresses the full realization of sin and unworthiness which precedes the coming of Grace. One might almost go so far as to say of *The Fall* what was said of Huysman's *À Rebours*—that the author now had to choose between conversion or suicide. A conversion by Camus would be a great triumph for the Catholic Church (it somehow seems unthinkable that a French writer might be converted to Protestantism), and Catholic critics have always adopted a most sympathetic and tolerant attitude towards Camus. It was hinted in several quarters that *The Rebel* might foreshadow a coming conversion. Even if *The Fall* is not followed by a conversion—and it does not at the moment look as if it will be—it nevertheless seems to be a book which, as Donat O'Donnell argued, might be read and understood in a Christian manner. The reader is told by Camus to identify the canals of Amsterdam with the concentric circles of hell, the title of the book is essentially religious, the obsession with man's unworthiness links it closely to the Catholic novels of Graham Greene or François Mauriac, and it seems to be a deeply felt cry *de profundis* for salvation.

Such an interpretation depends upon a close identification of the narrator with the author, and neglects one highly important possibility: that of irony. Camus has said that all his work is ironic, and he has also—in an essay entitled *L'Énigme*, published first in 1950 and reprinted in *L'Été*—protested against the tendency to identify him closely with the characters of his novels and particularly with the philosophy of the absurd. He said then that he would like to be an objective

writer who did not take himself as the subject for each one of
his books. It is also possible to interpret the name of the central
character in *The Fall* in another way, and thus to support the
interpretation of irony. Clamence is very near to the French
clémence (mercy, forgiveness)—precisely the quality which
Clamence most completely lacked. A clue to the real meaning
of *The Fall* may be found in an interview which Camus gave to
La Gazette Littéraire in March 1954. Speaking of his ideas on
original sin, he stated: 'People have insisted too much upon
the innocence of the creation. Now they want to crush us with
the feeling of our own guilt.' This is exactly what Clamence is
trying to do. When he tells the whole unpleasant truth about
himself, it is not in order to escape from his pride and find
refuge in true humility, but to make his listener accept that
what Clamence says of himself is also true of his own character. The aim of Clamence's demented but lucid monologue
is to present his listener with the Baudelairian idea of '*Hypocrite lecteur, mon semblable, mon frère*', and to convince him
of his own guilt. Clamence lovingly draws his own self-
portrait and then invites his listener to recognize his own
features in it. He has a motive in doing this which is made
quite clear at several points in the novel. His ambition has
always been to look down upon people from the heights of his
own virtue and perfection, and constantly to feel superior to
them. Once he had lost his complete self-assurance—as a
result of the discovery which he made of his own cowardice
when he did not rescue the young girl who jumped into the
Seine—he also lost his superiority and his ability to despise
others. He began to feel that people were laughing at him, and
seeing him as the '*pauvre type*' that he was terrified of being
taken for. Clamence had always been a monster of pride, and
when he could no longer feel that all other men were beneath
him as a result of his virtue, he was forced to subdue them by
making them feel their guilt. This is the explanation of his
strange calling of 'judge-penitent'.

Once he has managed to persuade his listener—who must,
as he himself admits, be an intelligent bourgeois like himself—
that all men are equally guilty, then his pride can once again be
satisfied:—'Covered with ashes, tearing my hair, my face
scored by clawing, but with piercing eyes, I stand before all
humanity recapitulating my own disgrace without losing sight

of the effect I am producing, and saying: "I was the lowest of the low." Then, imperceptibly, I pass from the "I" to the "We". When I get to the "This is what we are", the game is over and I can tell them all about themselves. I am just like them of course: we're all tarred with the same brush. However, I have a superiority in that I know it and this gives me the right to speak. You see the advantage, I am sure. The more I accuse myself, the more I have the right to judge you. Even better, I make you judge yourself, which makes it that much less necessary for me to do it.' It is solely in order to satisfy his passion for contempt that Clamence draws his listener into the trap of remorse and self-abasement. He exposes his reasons for doing so with as much clarity and openness as the Plague explains his motives in *State of Siege*, and there is a close similarity between the two characters.

Far from seriously expressing a belief in universal human wickedness in *The Fall*, Camus is satirising and attacking this belief. He sees it being used as a weapon for enslaving men, in the same way as in *The Rebel* he showed nihilism and the Marxist-Hegelian theory of history being used for the same purpose. This is quite obvious when Clamence is made to say, 'You see in me, *très cher*, an enlightened advocate of slavery.' There is little doubt that Clamence is a 'false prophet, crying in the wilderness and refusing to come forth', and that Camus intends what he says to be taken ironically. In *The Fall* Camus is far from denying the humanistic inspiration of his earlier work. He is attacking the idea of universal guilt by showing the despicable uses to which it may be put. He is in fact continuing the attack against slavery which formed one of the main themes of *The Rebel*, but is doing so from a different point of view and in a more subtle way. What he is principally attacking is the feeling of guilt which brings many middle-class intellectuals not only to Catholicism but also to communism. This is in keeping not only with the satirical intent of the book, but also with the works which came before it. And yet, in spite of the neatness with which it fits his earlier work, this explanation is not wholly satisfying.

The Fall was originally intended to form part of the collection of short stories, *Exile and the Kingdom*, which was first published in March 1957. These stories are set in different parts of the world—one in Brazil, one in France, the rest in

North Africa—and *The Fall* would have formed an excellent contrast by its evocation of the rain and mist of Amsterdam. However, as Camus worked upon it, the subject came to fascinate him more and more until it developed from a story into a short novel. It may be, of course, that the fascination which it exerted upon him was purely artistic, and that he became absorbed in the technical problem of making the psychology of Clamence both intelligible and acceptable. The short stories in *Exile and the Kingdom*, with their different styles of narration, are primarily exercises in technique which Camus is performing as preparation for writing a novel. It would therefore be quite reasonable for him to expand one of these stories into a short novel, if it seemed that the technique he was using was suited to this. Coupled, however, with the apparently strong autobiographical elements in it, and with the disquieting conviction of certain passages, the fact that Camus found the theme important enough to bear such an extensive development is rather significant. It is, in fact, possible that the story is not wholly satirical in nature, however much it may have been so in intention. Camus wrote it at the age of forty-three, the notorious middle of the journey, when the most sincere and assured men are said to go through a period of doubt and uncertainty. If *The Fall* is the *cri de coeur* of a humanistic writer who suddenly discovers—like Bernard Sands in *Hemlock and After*—that his motives are not so pure as he thinks, then this may account not only for its length but also for its considerable ambiguity. *The Fall* may be for Camus what *L'Immoraliste* and *La Porte étroite* were for André Gide —the opportunity to transcend certain problems through art and to liberate himself at the same time of certain personal obsessions. Like *L'Immoraliste* and *La Porte étroite*, *The Fall* gains much of its artistic excellence from its ambiguity. It is a disquieting book, more disquieting than anything else which Camus has written. A book that was purely ironic would not disturb the reader quite so much, and while it is not possible to accept Clamence as a wholly serious creation, he does incarnate an aspect of Camus's character which had remained hidden in his earlier works, and which he has exploited to its fullest extent. The short stories in *Exile and the Kingdom* are more controlled, but offer less interest to those who are interested primarily in what Camus thinks.

Donat O'Donnell suggested that one of the results of accepting seriously the ideas put forward in *The Fall* would be the impossibility of moral indignation. How, he asked, could a writer be indignant at the violence done to man when man himself was so undeserving of sympathy? *The Fall* has not, in fact, prevented Camus from expressing moral indignation, and in an interview published in *Encounter* in April 1957 he showed himself as horrified as any other intelligent person at the Russian barbarity in Hungary. He condemned it absolutely, and argued that all other intellectuals should do the same. He has not, however, voiced his protest through a work of art, as he did to a certain extent in 1947 with *The Plague*. The six stories in *Exile and the Kingdom* appear on first reading to be not only non-political but also non-metaphysical. Camus's work up to 1957 had been a meditation upon man, and upon his relationship with the world and with his fellows. His short stories are descriptions of men—and of women—rather than meditations upon them. Their importance lies in their value as works of art rather than in any hidden political or philosophical meaning which they may contain.

They all share, however, a central theme which is expressed in the title of the collection. All are studies in exile and in the attempt of people to find a country in which they will be fully at home. The first story *La Femme Adultère* (*The Woman taken in Adultery*) is the only one of Camus's works to have a woman as the chief character. Janine, the heroine of the story, is accompanying her husband on a trip to the wilder regions of North Africa where he is trying to sell cloth directly to the Arab merchants. She is impressed and attracted by the primitive life of the nomad tribesmen, with its dignity and freedom, and looking out over the desert from the walls of the town, she sees the tents of these 'poverty-stricken but free lords of a strange kingdom'. Somehow she feels this kingdom to be her own, and Camus writes: 'Janine did not know why this idea filled her with so sweet and vast a sadness that it made her shut her eyes. She knew only that this kingdom had been from all time promised to her, and yet that it would never belong to her, never again except perhaps for that fleeting moment when she opened her eyes once again on the suddenly motionless sky and its waves of coagulated light, while the voices rising from the Arab town grew suddenly silent. It seemed to her that the world had stopped turning and that from now onwards no one would die or grow old. At all places, henceforth, life was suspended, save there in her heart where, at that moment, someone was weeping with pain and wonderment.'

This nostalgia is mingled with the regret which she feels, as she grows heavy with approaching middle age, for the lightness and purity of her youth. The desire of Clamence in *The Fall*, for 'the sun, beaches and islands in the path of the trade winds, youth whose memory drives me to despair', parallels Janine's longing for her youth and the animal-like grace of the nomad tribesmen. But Janine escapes from her exile in the heavy body of her age, whereas Clamence cannot throw off his pride, guilt, and intellectual torment, and return to the happy islands of his guiltless youth (itself strangely reminiscent of Camus's own youth under the blinding sun of North Africa). At night, Janine steals out from her bedroom and climbs up again onto the terrace from which she had seen the tents of the nomads in the distance. There, like Meursault on the eve of his execution, she is 'opened to the tender indifference of the world'. She attains an almost sexual union with the earth and stars, a union in which she escapes from the cold and loneliness which have gripped her all day. 'No breeze and no noise, except from time to time the muffled cracking of the stones which the cold was splitting up into sand, disturbed the silence and solitude which lay about her. After a moment, however, she felt that the sky was sweeping down in a heavy movement over her head. In the depths of the dry, cold night, millions of stars came ceaselessly into being, while glittering icicles, falling immediately from them, began to slide irresistibly towards the horizon. Janine could not tear herself away from the contemplation of these drifting fires. She turned with them, and the same motionless journey reunited her little by little with her deepest being, where cold was now struggling with desire. In front of her, the stars fell one by one and then died out among the stones of the desert, and each time Janine opened herself a little further to the night. She breathed deeply, forgot the cold, the heaviness of human beings, the hysteria or boredom of life, the long anguish of living and of dying. After so many years in which, running away from fear, she had fled madly with no goal before her, she had at last come to rest. At the same time, she seemed to find her roots again, and the sap rose into her no longer trembling body. Striving towards the morning sky, her whole stomach pressed against the parapet, she waited only for her still thumping heart to grow quiet in its turn and for silence to reign within her. The last stars of the constellations dropped their clusters of light a little lower on the desert horizon, and remained motionless. Then, with an unbearable gentleness, the waters of the night began to fill Janine, drowning the cold, moving little by little from the dark core of her being, until they overflowed in uninterrupted waves right up into her mouth filled with groans. The next moment, the whole sky stretched over her as she lay with her back against the cold earth.'

Her 'adultery' consummated, weeping with relief, she stammers out to her husband as she lies in bed on her return: 'It's nothing, dear, nothing at all.'

Janine has, for a time, escaped from her exile into the kingdom which awaited her. She and the French engineer d'Arrast in the last story in the volume are the most fortunate of the characters in *Exile and the Kingdom*. They find their way into the country that they long for, and escape from the feeling of exile and solitude which is the dominant theme of this volume. Indeed, it is one of the permanent themes of Camus's work. The idea of separation comes in as a central preoccupation in *Cross-Purpose*, *The Plague*, and *The Just*, and is clearly a personal obsession with Camus himself. In Paris, he is in exile from his native Algeria, and in the bitter politics of modern France in exile from the land of justice of which he dreams. In *Nuptials*, one of the most moving images expresses his desire to unite land and sea on his own body, washing off the scents of one in the waves of the other. An almost Freudian yearning for union runs through practically the whole of his work, a longing for the country where contradictions will be resolved. It gives an emotional ring even to his philosophical writing, where, in *The Myth of Sisyphus*, the rejection of solutions is all the more moving as one is conscious of the longing which he has for reconciliation. If the short stories in *Exile and the Kingdom* tell us little about the evolution of Camus's ideas, they give us something much more valuable in their picture of the feeling of separation which has, directly or indirectly, inspired some of his most moving prose.

The second story in the collection, which was first published in review form in June 1956, is far more pessimistic in tone than *The Woman Taken in Adultery*, and is at first sight much more startling. It is written in the stream-of-consciousness manner which has been popularized in France far more by the novels of William Faulkner than by those of James Joyce or Virginia Woolf. Nevertheless, it would be assuming too much to say that Camus was directly influenced in it by Faulkner, although it was written at the same time as he was working on his adaptation of *Requiem for a Nun* for the French stage. Camus is a highly conscious literary artist, who chooses his techniques because of their suitability to the subject which he wants to treat, rather than because they are popular or because he has been deeply influenced by another writer. For example, his use of Hemingway's prose technique in *The Outsider* was due solely to the fact that he saw in it a convenient instrument for describing a man 'with no apparent consciousness of himself'. Similarly, the confusion of mind implicit in the stream-of-consciousness technique—in its first version the story was called *L'Esprit confus*—is exactly suited to the subject of the story. A rather stupid French missionary has gone out to what seems to be an extremely savage part of Africa—the actual place where the story is happening is not made clear—in order to try to convert a particularly barbarous tribe. The tribesmen have naturally refused to be converted, and have instead made the missionary a prisoner, cut out his tongue and castrated him. As a result of his privations, torture and imprisonment, the missionary has completely transformed the blind, unthinking allegiance which he had had for Christianity into an equally intolerant worship of the savages' idol, Râ. Determined now to serve this idol with the same absolute devotion that he had intended to serve Christ—but which had changed immediately into its opposite at his first real trial—the missionary has stolen an old rifle and escaped from his prison to wait in ambush for the priest who is coming to replace him. He shoots the priest, only to be killed himself by the tribesmen who have followed him to his ambush, and waited until he had done their work for them.

The story is told in a series of flashbacks, and the reader is obliged to piece the details together for himself. This is not, however, very difficult, as Camus's clarity of mind has not deserted him in this experiment in a new medium. The story can be made to fit into the theme of exile in several ways. The missionary is, of course, in a savage country far from his homeland, but more important than this is the fact that he has always been a stranger to true Christianity. It is made clear that his religion has been only a mask for his pride and for his power worship—'In fact,' he says, 'I had only understood that one thing, in my mulish intelligent way I went right to extremes, demanded all penances, was impatient with ordinary things, yes, I wanted to be an example, I too, so that people could see me and on seeing me would pay homage to what had made me better, in me and through me salute the Saviour. ... Powerful, yes, that was the word that I endlessly rolled around my tongue, I dreamed of absolute power, dreamed of being him who brings the others to their knees, forces the enemy to capitulate, finally converts him, and the more the enemy is blind, cruel, sure of himself, buried in his own certainty, the more his confession proclaims the regal power of him who has caused his defeat.'

It is his worship of power which has caused him so easily to deny Christianity and turn to the blind obedience of the savages' idol, whom he now proclaims to be all-powerful. In a way, he illustrates one of the ideas expressed in *The Rebel*—that he who rebels completely will be most easily tempted by complete conformity to a new set of absolute and intolerant values. It may be that the story is an allegory of the Christian intellectual who gives up Christianity for communism because of the longing which he has for power and because of his basic attitude of power-worship—an idea which recalls George Orwell's diagnosis of the attraction which communism has for many intellectuals. But the point of the story does not lie in the possibility of any allegorical meaning which it might contain, but in the picture which it gives of a particular psychological case. It shows a perception of the true nature of intolerance as well as, indirectly, an understanding of the Christian virtue of humility. It stands out from the other stories in this volume by its extreme physical violence—once again a feature of all forms of intolerance.

Les Muets (*Silence*) is in complete contrast to the first two stories, both in its subject matter and its style. It is written in a direct, realistic prose which differs from the impressionistic and poetic style of *The Woman taken in Adultery* and from the

interior monologue of *Le Renégat* (*The Betrayal*). It too is set
in North Africa, and its central character, Yvars, is clearly an
older and sadder version of the Vincent whom Camus had
admired in *Nuptials* for his simple, instinctive love of life.
Contrasting Vincent's straightforward sensuality with the
complicated exploitation of the senses in Gide—whom Camus
did not greatly admire in this respect—he wrote: 'My friend
Vincent, who is a cooper and junior swimming champion, has
a clearer view of things. He drinks when he is thirsty, if he
wants a woman tries to go to bed with her, and would marry
her if he were in love with her (this hasn't happened yet).
Afterwards, he always says; "That's much better," which is a
vigorous summing up of the apologia which one might write
in defence of satisfaction.' Yvars is a cooper and, since he is
lame in one leg, has always been fond of swimming. He might
well be Camus's boyhood friend, now past his prime, and
barely managing to make a living in an industry which is
dying out. Camus had written in *Nuptials* that, in North
Africa, a working man who was over thirty had already had all
his fun from life, and had to resign himself to taking second
place before the tempestuous young. He is now studying the
same fact twenty years later, and from a necessarily more sober
and pessimistic point of view. Yvars still likes to look at the
sea, remembering 'the deep, clear water, the strong sun, the
girls, the life of the body—there being no other happiness in
this country, and this happiness disappeared with youth', but
now prefers to look out over the sea only when it changes
colour in the cool of the evening. In the morning, as he pedals
to work on his bicycle, he prefers to look in the opposite
direction.

Yvars and his friends have held a strike, but have been
forced to go back without obtaining the increase they had
asked for. In the workshop they refuse, partly through pride
and partly through humiliation, to reply to the owner when he
comes in and tries to talk to them. Then, in the afternoon of
the same day, the owner's little daughter falls seriously ill and
has to be taken away in an ambulance. As the men are preparing to go home, the owner comes into the workshop again.
This time, it is shyness and not deliberate intention which
prevents the men from replying. Some sort of contact has been
re-established, but Yvars is made to feel how deeply each one

of the acts which we perform involves us with the feelings of other people. That evening, as he looks out over the sea, he wishes he were young again and could sail away to the other side of the sea. *Tony analysis - years' story.*

In *Silence*, Camus's technique is close to that of Joyce in *Dubliners*, with the selection of an isolated incident and its treatment in an inconclusive way. It is only his refusal to treat his subject in detail which enables him to avoid the sentimentality inherent in such a theme. Here the exile is the inevitable conflict between men—which destroys the contact between the employees and the owner, whom they all quite like in the normal run of things—while the kingdom is the unity of all men in family affection, illness and suffering. The story is a melancholy one, not only in its theme of the failure to make contact, but also in its treatment of the loss of youth. Together with the slightly satirical *Jonas, ou l'Artiste au Travail*, it is the most autobiographical of the short stories. Camus's fidelity to North Africa and to the happiness of his youth there is one of the strongest features of his work. Now that he is middle-aged, and his native Algeria the centre of bloodshed and violence, his feeling of exile is made more acute. The next story, *L'Hôte* (*The Guest*), introduces the reader into one of the many problems which face the French resident in present-day Algeria. Camus has been widely criticized for his silence on the Algerian question. Although he has protested against the French home government's misuse of power—particularly in the arrest, in May 1956, of journalists who had been in contact with the rebel leaders—he has adopted a far less belligerent attitude than Sartre. It is possible that *The Guest* is an attempt to express the personal difficulties which he himself experiences in judging the Algerian situation.

Daru, a French schoolmaster born in Algeria—'anywhere else, he felt himself in exile'—is alone in his school on a high plateau, almost cut off by a sudden fall of snow. The local gendarme, Balducci, comes to the school on horseback, bringing with him as a prisoner an Arab who, in a family quarrel, has killed one of his cousins with a hedging hook. Daru is told that he has to escort this Arab to the police station 15 miles away, in order to avoid the trouble which is brewing up in the Arab's village. He is unwilling to do this, but is obliged to accept custody of the Arab, and does so with the intention of allowing him to escape. During the night which the Arab spends in the school, he feeds and looks after him, refuses to tie him up, and is disappointed that he does not escape during the night. The next morning, Daru takes him to a point from where he can walk either towards the town where the prison awaits him, or towards the desert where the nomad tribes will shelter him. He gives him food that will enable him to make the day's journey into the desert, and leaves him to choose. As he looks back, the Arab is marching towards the town.

On his return, through the strong sunlight which is drying up the snow, Daru finds that an uneducated hand has scrawled across the blackboard: 'You have handed over our brother. You will pay for it ...' The story closes with the sentence: 'In this enormous country which he had loved so much, he was alone.'

The Guest is a story of <u>misunderstanding</u> and of unhappy accident, and a much deeper study of the same theme than the play *Cross-Purpose*. Daru wants to do good, and seems to symbolize the generous and civilizing aspects of French administration. It is he, we are told, who has the task of distributing the corn sent by France to save the Arabs from famine when their crops fail through drought. He is horrified at the stupid crime which the Arab has committed, and refuses his invitation to leave the school and join the rebel bands. The Arab himself is hardly conscious of what is happening, is incapable of understanding that a European could offer him his freedom, and quite unable to live outside the narrow community which he has now had to leave. Daru's generosity is misinterpreted because the rebels judge only on appearances and refuse to see that Europeans can do any good except by joining the Arab rebel movements. If the story has any message, it is an appeal for understanding and for tolerance on all sides. Daru is tempted to hate men—'this man, all men, and their dirty wickedness, their untiring hatred, their mad thirst for blood'—but cannot bring himself to hand over a man for execution. His dilemma is that of the many French residents in Algeria who are unable to bear violence but unable to live elsewhere than in the country where they were born and have made their home. It is the tragedy of exiles in a country which used to be their own which the 'minor incident' of *The Guest* expresses.

The order in which the short stories are presented has been carefully thought out by Camus. Coming immediately after the two short, realistically described, rather sad stories of *Silence* and *The Guest*, the leisurely irony of *Jonah or the Artist at Work* provides a slackening of tension before the final story gathers together the ideas of exile and of belonging, and expresses them in a final synthesis. *Jonah* is the most amusing story which Camus has so far written. Modern French writers, acutely conscious of the need to express the spirit of the times, have naturally avoided writing humorous books. If there is any humour in their work, it is the *humour noir* which the Surrealists found in the Marquis de Sade and Alfred Jarry. There are elements of humour in Camus's earlier work—especially in *The Outsider* and in the opening descriptions of *The Plague*—but it is of a rather ironic kind. In *Jonah* the humour is more gentle and more genuinely amusing, in spite of the basically serious intention of the story. Jonah is a painter, and is in fact interested in nothing but painting. He has faith in his star, which he knows will bring him good fortune, and he is not disappointed. But as he becomes more and more famous, the small flat in which he lives—which is delightfully described—is invaded by a host of friends and of disciples, so that it becomes increasingly difficult for him to paint any more at all. He is presented with petitions and with foreign celebrities, invited to lunch and dinner, and con- stantly surrounded by disciples who 'explain to him at great length what he has painted and why.' Under their guidance, Jonah discovers in his work 'many intentions which surprised him a little, and a multitude of things which he had not put there', but he does not find their presence very helpful to his actual painting. The host of visitors, disciples and critics who add to the noise and confusion made by his wife and three children, and by the incessant ringing of the telephone, drive Jonah from one room to another in search of somewhere peaceful where he will be able to paint. Finally, he constructs a kind of attic in a high corner of his flat, and retreats there alone. After many days of quiet meditation, during which he sees only his friend Radeau, and eats practically nothing, he falls ill. On the one canvas on which he has been working is written, in tiny characters, a single word. His friend Radeau cannot make out whether this word is '*solidaire*' or '*solitaire*'.

While this story is primarily a humorous evocation, in an almost Paul Jennings style, of the difficulties of a man who has to work at home, and of the particular difficulties of an amiable artist in a critic-infested community, it has a serious theme: that of the relationship between the artist and the community. The idea which Camus expresses at the very end is that the artist or writer is most '*solidaire*'—that is, in communion with his time—when he is most solitary. Or, in other words, it is impossible to tell an artist that he must try deliberately to come into contact with real life, and live surrounded by the same preoccupations as ordinary men. If he is a true artist, the contact will be made through his art, however lonely he may be—or appear to be—during the actual process of artistic creation. It is difficult to see the precise meaning of the title of the story, and especially of the quotation from Jonah, i. 12—'And he said unto them, Take me up and cast me forth into the sea ... for I know that for my sake this great tempest is upon you'—which Camus places at the very beginning. One possible interpretation is that as Jonah is left less and less alone, he is less and less able to paint, and thus to gain the livelihood of those who are dependent upon him—an interpretation which underlines the need to provide the artist with a certain isolation if he and that part of society which depends upon him are to survive. In any case, these 'meanings' which can be read into it are incidental to the story itself, which is above all an ironic commentary—almost certainly drawn from personal experience—of the dangers surrounding a famous artist or writer in the modern world. It is also a polite and amusing warning to Camus's critics, imitators, and those who choose to write books about him.

The last story in the volume—*La Pierre qui Pousse* (*The Growth of a Stone*)—was announced as a forthcoming publication in the *Nouvelle Nouvelle Revue Française* as early as 1954. The first draft of one section—*Une Macumba au Brésil*—appeared in 1951, but was much altered before being made part of the story. This is rather heavily descriptive, and tells of the arrival and experiences of a French engineer, d'Arrast, in the small Brazilian town of Iguape where he has gone to organize the building of a dam. He has left Europe, where there is only 'shame and anger', but finds that he cannot adapt himself to the primitive life in the new world. He strikes up a curious friendship with a ship's cook, who tells him of a vow that he has made to Christ, if he should be saved from a shipwreck. He has promised that he will carry a heavy stone on his head all the way to the church on the local saint's day. Unfortunately, he is possessed by a fury for dancing at the more pagan ceremony which is held on the eve of the saint's day, and is too exhausted the next morning to be able to fulfil his promise. When he falls down under the weight of the stone, d'Arrast picks it up for him and carries it on his own head to the hut where the cook lives with the rest of his family. There, the family sit around and gaze at the stone which d'Arrast has placed in the centre of the floor. After a silence, d'Arrast is invited to sit down with them, and he does so, happy at having found a place where he once again belongs.

The book closes on this image, and on the idea which has run through Camus's work from the first essays of *Betwixt and Between*. There, he described how he was torn between the feeling of natural union and identification with the world, and the love for his fellow men which took him away from it. It is this division in his character which the French critic Roger Quillot has expressed in his book on Camus's work entitled *La Mer et les Prisons*. Camus's difficulty, like that of d'Arrast, is one of entering into contact with other men without abdicating his own liberty or losing his individuality. D'Arrast cannot sacrifice his intelligence and join the natives of Iguape in the wild dancing through which they quite forget their own individuality, any more than he can live in his own country where 'the rulers are merchants or policemen'. He has come to serve men in a simple and practical way by building a dam, in the same way as Rieux had served them by treating their sick bodies. Yet he does not enter into emotional and satisfying contact with them until he has deliberately assumed a task which has no practical value but an immense spiritual significance—the carrying of a heavy stone as an act of religious gratitude. He does not carry it into the church, but back to his friend's home. He can share religious feeling but not religious faith; the stone is still there for his friend to carry again, without suffering a sense of failure and humiliation. The figure of Sisyphus has turned up again in a different form. In a grotto in the town of Iguape, there is a miraculous stone which grows a little more out of the rock every year. D'Arrast goes to see the pilgrims waiting to break off a piece of this miraculous rock, and feels that he has almost found what he has been waiting for during the whole of his long travels in Brazil. He does not, however, find this until he picks up the rock which his friend was carrying and places it on his own head. Service to man, Camus is saying, depends not upon the acceptance of miracles, but upon the assumption of tasks which may seem to be absurd, but which are in fact full of significance.

At the beginning of *The Rebel*, Camus indicates the theme of the book by giving a quotation from Hölderlin: 'And openly I vowed my heart to the grave and suffering earth, and often, in the sacred night, I promised to love it faithfully until death, without fear, with its heavy burden of fatality, and to despise none of its enigmas. Thus I bound myself to it with an immortal link.' The same idea of service and of an attempt at comprehension runs through the stories in *Exile and the Kingdom*. Indeed, this book seems at times the attempt to express the same attitude towards life which Camus described in *The Rebel*, but in a much more indirect and modest way. He was not himself fully satisfied with *The Rebel* as a work of art, and has possibly realized that it is extremely difficult to present his own primarily emotional attitude towards life in such highly philosophical arguments. *Exile and the Kingdom* gives in fact the impression that Camus has begun a genuinely new period of creative activity. By 1951, he had come to the impasse which threatens any liberal humanistic writer at the present time. He was certain of the values which he wishes to express—justice, tolerance, freedom of thought, an empirical approach towards political problems—but unable either to express these values directly through a work of art or to make any decisive contribution to their realization in political life. It is impossible to create works of art by repeating moral truths, however admirable and salutary these may be. Two possibilities remain, and Camus has exploited both of them in *The Fall* and in *Exile and the Kingdom*. One is to satirize modes of thought which menace the values which he holds dear, the other to show human beings in actual situations in which these values are necessary but difficult to realize. Insofar as Camus's work continues to be concerned with the expression of certain ideas, it is likely that these will be expressed indirectly through the medium of the novel and the short story, rather than directly through philosophical essays. The symbolism of *Jonah* seems to indicate that it is through his individual creation as an artist that Camus now considers himself most likely to give expression to the problems of his time. In a letter in August 1956 he wrote: 'The truth is that I consider myself first and foremost as an artist, and that problems of style and composition never cease to preoccupy me, especially when I refuse to cut myself off from the questions of our day.' It must be remembered that *Exile and the Kingdom* is first and foremost a set of exercises in the technique of story-telling, a preparation for a novel which he is beginning to write. Like André Gide, Camus is acutely conscious that the word 'novel' should be applied only to works of art which satisfy certain conditions. So far, he has not used the word to describe any one of his works. *The Outsider* and *The Fall* are both '*récits*' and *The Plague* is a '*chronique*'. In none of them is there the necessary depth and complexity to justify the word 'novel'. Until this novel appears it will not be possible to judge of the complete success or failure of the creative revival in Camus's work. Neither *The Fall* nor *Exile and the Kingdom* can really bear comparison with *The Outsider* or *The Plague* as major works of art. They are, in a way, similar to the essays of *Nuptials* and *Betwixt and Between*. Any judgment of Camus's achievement so far must be based essentially on the books of his 'philosophical period', at the same time as we remember that his career as a creative artist is possibly only just beginning.

CHAPTER SEVEN

ACHIEVEMENT AND LIMITATIONS

IN 1950, shortly before she died, Rachel Bespaloff wrote the following judgment of Camus's work up to that date. 'A short treatise, two stories, a drama, a tragedy, a few letters, few pages, few words, but, in these few, modern man and his torment, his sin and his grandeur.' Her opinion is representative of the attitude adopted by the majority of Camus's French admirers—who are numerous—and it provides a convenient starting-point for a summing up of his achievement so far. It insists upon the metaphysical rather than on the aesthetic value of his work and claims more for him, perhaps, than most English readers would allow. Seen from the outside, and from a different philosophical and emotional atmosphere, the limitations of Camus's work are obvious. They are most apparent in his two philosophical essays, less so in his plays, and least of all in his poetic prose and his novels. It is perhaps as well to express criticism first, and to begin by those of his works which I personally find least satisfying—*The Myth of Sisyphus* and *The Rebel*.

The Myth of Sisyphus suffers from the fact that it is a presentation of an emotional experience in supposedly rational and philosophical terms. It is when it is examined from a philosophically critical standpoint that the weaknesses of the 'essay on the absurd' are most apparent. To begin with, as A. J. Ayer has pointed out, Camus's 'proof' of the absurdity of the world is most unsatisfying. For example, Camus uses a traditional argument from Aristotle in order to show the world's incomprehensibility. No one, he writes, has given a more elegant proof of the mind's incapacity for distinguishing truth from falsehood. If I affirm that everything is true, I affirm the truth of the contradictory statement, and thus the falseness of my own original statement, for its contradiction implies that it cannot be true. If, on the other hand, I say that nothing is true, this also is wrong, for I cannot say that only the statement which contradicts my own is false without being obliged at the same time to admit the possibility that other statements may be true. A. J. Ayer wrote of this argument that, while it was an ingenious piece of philosophical reasoning, it proved nothing at all about the absurdity of the world. 'All that it proves,' he wrote, 'is that the terms of truth and falsehood cannot be significantly applied to the totality of all propositions ...' and argued that in order for Camus's requirements for a rational world to be satisfied, matters of fact would have to be logically necessary. Camus, in making this demand, is expressing what modern English philosophers would call 'a pointless lament' and asking for the impossible. Similarly, if one examines the illustration taken from modern physics, it simply reveals that Camus is requiring the world to be intelligible in the terms of the absolute necessities of nineteenth-century mechanistic physics. The more personal example of the man finding his train of thought interrupted is a proof of nothing but of the fact that we are so physiologically and psychologically constituted that our conscious mind is not always working. To require that it should be is once again to put forward a theory of the nature of consciousness which does not correspond to the facts. In *The Myth of Sisyphus*, Camus is asking for the philosophically impossible. The reader is far less convinced of the absurdity of the world after having read the opening pages of *The Myth of Sisyphus* than after reading *The Outsider* or *Betwixt and Between*. Camus is acutely and emotionally aware of the absurd, but is unable to communicate this awareness in rational and persuasive terms. He does, himself, in the preface to *The Myth of Sisyphus*, speak of 'the feeling of the absurd', and it is this feeling rather than an exact and convincing notion which he succeeds in expressing.

Where his essay is more satisfying as a piece of reasoning is in the development of its arguments and in the general attitude towards life which Camus deduces from them. This attitude is attractive and, within certain limits, a highly valid one. It is, moreover, an attitude which is based upon a philosophically valid idea and one upon which it is salutary to insist. The fact that reason cannot give a satisfactory reply to all questions is no excuse for abandoning it entirely and plunging into the nearest convenient mystical explanation. Since science—or rather scientific philosophy—lost its nineteenth-century assurance and admitted that in many cases it could not be absolutely certain of things, religious thinkers have tended to proclaim that, 'reason being useless', man should therefore return to the true faith, accept authority, and worship because he cannot understand. It is almost the same idea which Camus convincingly refutes in the thinkers he denounces in *The Myth of Sisyphus*. Even though his premiss of the absurdity of the world may be highly personal and unproven, his attitude towards it is most consistent. Basically, it is the traditional Protestant cry of 'By what judgment can I judge but by mine own?' revived in the context of a new set of thinkers, and linked with a modest realization that although reason and individual judgment may be fallible, they are in fact all we have.

To deduce a hedonistic attitude to life from the meaningless-ness of the world is a movement as old as philosophy. To couple it, as Camus does, with a cult of intensity and of the lucid main-tenance of consciousness, brings a corrective dignity to what might easily become mere pleasure-seeking. The English reader nurtured upon Browning, Kipling and Chesterton, or the Frenchman infused with the spirit of Péguy or Vigny, here breathes a familiar and a bracing moral air. Camus divests the cult of effort for its own sake from the moral trimmings of the nineteenth century, and sees it as a pure witness to man's dig-nity. To strive on without the assumptions of nineteenth-century optimism, the Public School code or the ultimate justification of Catholicism is an infinitely nobler thing even than to be inspired by a heroic but a certain faith. It may be useless, as one French critic put it, 'to keep one's eyes passionately open in the dark-ness', but it is surely better, and possibly more profitable, than to close them and trust in someone else's reports of a guiding light.

This, is, however, a feature of Camus's thought most appreci-ated by those already prejudiced in favour of scepticism, and hostile to the irrational paradoxes of religion. The ultimate value of Camus's attitude may be contested, but not its consistency. The essential quality of *The Myth of Sisyphus*, admirably reflected in its style and in its construction, lies in the rigorous development of Camus's arguments. Throughout the book he insists upon the fact that he is striving only towards a provisional attitude, but that this attitude must be consistent with the premises from which he starts out. One may question Camus's premises, but not the way in which he reaches his conclusions once these premises are temporarily accepted. Deliberately contrasting in every way with *The Outsider*, while at the same time expressing the same experience and attitude towards life, *The Myth of Sisyphus* is a network of explanations and explanatory phrases. Its effect upon the reader, however, is, curiously enough, very similar to that of the novel—it obliges him to enter into an autonomous world, and to be caught up in a pattern of arguments and experiences, from which he can escape only by a deliberate effort of conscious criticism. The continual repetition in *The Myth of Sisyphus* of similar phrases expressing perseverance—'it's simply a question of tenacity', 'here we must be persistent', 'it is this that we must hang on to', 'I want to repeat it yet again'—indicates the whole aim of the essay: to reach a provisional solution which will be consistent and legitimate while allowing for an authentic development. Camus does not judge Jaspers, Kierkegaard or Chestov from a rationalist viewpoint but from that of the absurd. In the same way as his fidelity to revolt enables him, in *The Rebel*, to judge those thinkers who have betrayed it, so his insistence on the true nature of the absurd allows him to point out that those who use it as a springboard into religion are intellectually unjustified. Camus's perseverance in *The Myth of Sisyphus*, and the way in which he obstinately returns and sticks to the terms of the problem as he understands and defines it, make the essay extraordinarily fascinating to read. They produce a kind of *envoûtement* while at the same time they exalt consciousness and provide a most satisfying unity. The whole effort of *The Myth of Sisyphus* is to maintain an attitude of refusal and obstinate perseverance, and this idea is reflected in the style and in the construction. It is not only in novels that technique reflects a metaphysic, but also, in certain privileged cases, in philosophical essays.

The idea of the absurd, as Camus expresses it in *The Myth of Sisyphus*, is associated not only with this stubborn perseverance, but also with a cult of tension and contrast. These qualities are likewise reflected in the style which Camus uses. He speaks of the effort to '*soutenir le pari merveilleux et déchirant de l'absurde*' of living in '*un univers brûlant et glacé, transparent et limité, où rien n'est possible mais où tout est donné*'. In this world, existence is at one and the same time '*mensongère et éternelle*', of infinite value precisely because it is finite in time. His style brings out the effort of lucidity and the tension of living in this world where consciousness is a perpetual defiance and effort of revolt, and where, paradoxically, happiness springs from despair. It is a world from which God is exiled, and where destiny is a human affair, '*qui doit être réglée entre les hommes*'. Camus's style enables him to express this revolt, and the love of man which results necessarily from it, without falling into any sentimentality. His early humanism, like his style, is virile, intense and proud. The '*univers farouche et limité de l'homme*' is brought unexpectedly to life in this philosophical essay through the creation of an autonomous world by an individual style. It is in the prose of *The Myth of Sisyphus* that Camus's humanism finds its most moving expression. In the passage on the Conqueror, he writes:

'*Oui, l'homme est sa propre fin. Et il est sa seule fin. S'il veut être quelque chose, c'est dans cette vie. ... Visages tendus, fraternité menacée, amitié si forte et si pudique des hommes entre eux, ce sont les vraies richesses parce qu'elles sont périssables. C'est au milieu d'elles que l'esprit sent le mieux ses pouvoirs et ses limites.*'

'Yes, man is his own end, and he is himself the only end to which he can aspire. If he wants to be something, it is in this life. ... Tense faces, fraternity in danger, the shy strong friendship of men for men, these are true riches because they are mortal. It is in the midst of them that the mind feels best its limits and its powers.'

In *The Outsider* and *The Myth of Sisyphus*, Camus is most completely and most convincingly the anti-Pascal, the author whose hero finds life so fully satisfying that he would be happy to spend the rest of it simply in one room. It is when reading *The Myth of Sisyphus* that one understands fully the reasons why Camus has so repeatedly stated that he is *not* an existentialist, for the existentialist attitude, from Job to Kierkegaard through Pascal, has always been to deny the competence of man to decide his own destiny.

Camus has denied that he is a philosopher. 'What interests me,' he writes, 'is how one should behave.' Certainly, for a hostile critic, the weakness of parts of *The Myth of Sisyphus* underlines the truth of this statement. What Camus meant by it is that he cannot reason abstractly about a subject on which he does not feel, or has not felt, intensely. Thus, in his work up to the present, there has been no treatment of the traditional philosophical problems of time and space, of causality, of free will and determinism, of appearance and reality. Unlike the professional or academic philosopher, he writes only of what he knows from personal experience. It is as a record of personal experience, expressed in an artistically satisfying way, that *The Myth of Sisyphus* is principally to be valued. It is when read in company with the directly emotional presentation of the experience of the absurd in *The Outsider*, in *Betwixt and Between* and in *Nuptials* that the illustrations in the very first part of the book are most persuasive. The considerable success of the essay at the time of publication—and in the immediate post-war period—was due very much to the fact that in insisting upon the absurdity of the world, Camus was expressing the historical experience of his generation. Few of his French critics, then or now, have questioned the assumptions with which *The Myth of Sisyphus* begins. These critics were, themselves, too involved in a situation which was both implicitly and explicitly absurd, to be able to discuss critically Camus's assumptions. It needed an academic philosopher like Ayer, writing in an English intellectual atmosphere little affected by the circumstances which dominated French thinking, quietly to point out how unproven these assumptions were. In *The Myth of Sisyphus* Camus's rationalization of his own personal experiences foreshadowed the historical development of the Europe of the forties, in the same way as Kafka's own private universe revealed itself to be the expression of '*la condition humaine*' in the mid-twentieth century. Bespaloff's remark seems then to apply most readily to *The Myth of Sisyphus* when the essay is considered in the intellectual and emotional atmosphere of a Europe in despair and defeat. Insofar as the Europe of 1957 has emerged from this despair, the expression which *The Myth of Sisyphus* gives of man's lot seems, to the English middle-class reader of 1957, to be less exact. There is, however, an element of more permanent truth in Camus's description of contemporary man, which is particularly evident in passages like the following: 'Sometimes the décor collapses. Get up, ride on the bus, work four hours in an office or factory, get on the bus, have a meal, get on the bus, work four hours, have a meal, go to bed and Monday Tuesday Wednesday Thursday Friday Saturday on the same rhythm—the road is easily followed most of the time. But one day, the question of "why" comes into it, and everything begins in this weariness tinged with amazement.' The condition of the vast majority of the working population is still precisely that, and it is strange that a book which deals with such apparently esoteric figures as Jaspers and Husserl should at the same time express it so exactly. As an honest confrontation of the problem of the meaninglessness of the world, and a presentation of a consistent attitude to be adopted towards it, *The Myth of Sisyphus* is, after fifteen years, an acute and up-to-date book. Even if, in a hundred years' time, human life seems to possess a greater degree of meaning, *The Myth of Sisyphus* will still be readable for its style and for its construction.

The ambition of *The Rebel* to explain the failure of revolutions over the last hundred and fifty years to attain their objects is a considerable one, and must be held to account for much of the unsatisfactory nature of the book. *The Myth of Sisyphus* was more modest, and considerably more successful in its more limited aims. Although Rachel Bespaloff wrote her judgment upon Camus before *The Rebel* was published, there is no doubt that she would have extended it to cover his second long philosophical essay. It is, indeed, with the lot of modern man that *The Rebel* is concerned. It is, however, concerned with him only inasmuch as he is a political animal inspired in his political actions by philosophy. Camus devotes whole sections of *The Rebel* to Hegel, Marx, Saint-Just and Nietzsche, illustrating them by studies of Rimbaud, Sade, the surrealists, Dostoievsky and Blake, in order to explain why revolutions end up by betraying their ideals. The instinctive reaction of the English reader is to reread *Animal Farm*, and to agree wholeheartedly with those of Camus's critics who took him to task for not discussing the economic and social origins of revolution, or the actual circumstances in which they take place. The book is certainly unbalanced in the immense importance which it gives to thinkers and the small amount of actual historical analysis which it contains. It is also unsatisfying and, in the long run, a rather annoying book, because it is almost exclusively a work of destructive criticism. Camus never speaks of any revolt or revolution which even partially succeeded. Nothing seems to matter to him outside the French Revolution or the coming of Russian communism. To an Anglo-Saxon reader this is strange, and detracts from the comprehensiveness of Camus's attempt to understand the time he lives in by examining it from the point of view of revolt and revolution. Surely the experience of England in the second half of the seventeenth century, of America in the eighteenth, of England again at the very time when Camus was writing *The Rebel*, are relevant to the ideas he is discussing? Here at least are revolutions which, although no one would claim that they were absolutely successful, did avoid the danger which Camus finds in other revolts—the passage to military dictatorship. Moreover, they do represent an effort to realize those essentially limited aims which Camus finds as representative of true revolt. The fact that he does not even mention them is due partly to the rather parochial tradition of revolt which he is studying, and partly to his instinctive distrust of official liberal democracy. Yet it is strange, as R. H. S. Crossman pointed out, that Camus should ignore not only the bourgeois tradition of revolt, but also only mention in passing the history of the British and American labour parties. Not only does Camus not discuss relatively successful revolts on the political plane, but he also fails to give any example of an author who rebelled against his time or against things as he found them, and whose revolt did not reflect the nihilism which Camus is attacking. There are, nevertheless, examples of such writers— Shaw, Voltaire, Péguy, Malraux, Ibsen, Freud, Zola, Bernanos, to mention but a few—and the complete omission of their names gives the book a lop-sided character. It is certainly justified and necessary to denounce a current of nihilism which masquerades as revolt, but the attack against it is likely to be more effective if examples are given of other writers who avoided this danger. Otherwise, the book appears very much like the lament of a prophet crying in the wilderness. If *The Rebel* does give this impression, it is not because there are in fact no other traditions of revolt which Camus can oppose to the one he is criticizing, but simply because he does not choose to do so. His book conse-quently lacks the comprehensiveness which would make of it something more than an attack against a rather limited nihilist tradition, whose importance for the development of history Camus exaggerates. While it presents only a very partial view of the question, *The Rebel* does not have the compensatory quality of many other insufficient studies of communism—the violence and effectiveness of a satire. Camus's tone of superior intel-lectual investigation and of scrupulous attention to detail—a tone which is not justified by the completeness of the book—deprives it of the life and vigour which would make up for its insufficiencies. This can possibly be best brought out by comparing Camus with George Orwell, whose attack on communism is even narrower, intellectually, than Camus's, but is more effective as literature.

Camus sees communism as perverted by the influence of a particular philosophy, while Orwell sees it as betrayed by man's wickedness and lust for power. Both viewpoints provide insufficient explanations of its nature, and both do so through over-simplification. In Orwell's case, however, the attack is made in a medium which is necessarily suited to over-simplification—that of the satire. Orwell interrupts Winston Smith's reading of Goldstein's book at the moment when the final explanation seems to be forthcoming. 'I understand the "how",' writes Orwell. 'It is the "why" which I cannot understand.' Were *The Rebel* a more comprehensive work, it could well accompany *Nineteen Eighty-Four*, explaining the 'why' just as Orwell showed, through his realistic satire, the 'how'. Unfortunately, it does not do this. Orwell is more effective than Camus as a critic of communism precisely because he is a horrified and irrational one, and because he does not attempt to provide a rational explanation. He is in the tradition of satire, where, as in Swift, hatred lends force and compulsion. Like Swift, he creates a powerful and biting satire through the combination of a brilliant intellectual idea and a number of powerful, physical obsessions. Camus does something similar in *The Plague*, though not in the medium of satire, and makes the reader share the force of his conviction. In *The Rebel*, however, unless the reader is familiar with the nihilist and philosophical tradition which Camus is criticizing, the attack against communism is obscured in a mass of philosophical and literary detail. It is true that Camus is trying to do much more than Orwell. He is trying to explain, where Orwell is merely describing. It is right, however, that he should be judged by higher standards. If a work professes to be 'an effort to understand my time', it is legitimate to criticize it for providing a very one-sided explanation.

This is not to say that many of the points which Camus makes are not valid, or that his book is completely irrelevant to the real situation. A study of the philosophy of revolutions is most important at a time when the philosophers have, for the first

time in history, exercised so great an influence. It is one of
Camus's noblest characteristics—his refusal to believe that men
are naturally wicked—which leads him to the over-simplification
which is the main fault of *The Rebel*. Since men are good, the
evil they do comes from the fact that they are misled. A philosopher must therefore be found whose influence is likely to have
misled them. Hegel is conveniently there as a philosopher who
influenced certain early communists and whose thought can be
used to justify almost any political pretensions. He is therefore,
argues Camus, responsible for the crimes which communism
commits. It is certainly necessary to point out that philosophies
do mislead men and that the Hegelian philosophy implies the
sacrifice of the individual to historical progress. To suggest,
however, as Camus does in *The Rebel*, that this philosophy is
responsible for the suppression and sacrifice of the individual is
to give to a philosophy an exclusive importance which history,
economics, geography, and the nature of man cannot but deny
it. Camus's attack on communism is valid up to a point, but that
point is soon reached. His is not a particularly original criticism.
Koestler's Roubashov, meditating on his past career and on his
present condemnation, found that a worship of history was one
of the causes which had led him to betray others and to be himself accused. Koestler does not, however, suggest that this
worship of history is the only reason, and his criticism of the
communist doctrine is the more telling for it.

In addition to these weaknesses, *The Rebel* does not possess
the compensatory qualities of construction and style which are
to be found in *The Myth of Sisyphus*. In the essay on the absurd,
Camus's constant return to the same idea was fully justified by
the fact that the work was an effort to reach a reply to a question
by rigorous examination of certain thinkers. There, the fact that
he everywhere found the same refusal to confront reality and to
escape by *l'esquive* (evasion) confirmed the validity of his central
argument. In *The Rebel*, however, the central idea of nihilism
has become such an obsession that Camus is often prevented
from seeing the real value of the authors he discusses. While it is
true, as he pointed out in the quarrel with André Breton, that he
had praised Rimbaud and surrealism, the fact remains that his
treatment of Rimbaud, Lautréamont and Sade is extremely
superficial. He sees them all as a doctor sees his patients and diag-
noses the same illness in each one of them. Instead of allowing

that Rimbaud's farewell to poetry may well have been an attempt to attain reality by other means, an inevitable result of mere adolescent impatience, or an intensely honest attempt at moral repentance—similar to that of Marlowe's Faust—he sees it as yet another manifestation of nihilism. He disregards the considerable possibility that Lautréamont's apparent *volte-face* may in fact have been a mere attempt at irony, and completely neglects the fact that Sade's peculiar sexual temperament, rather than his yearning for the absolute, led him to wish to imprison his victims far from the sight of men. His treatment of Nietzsche is certainly more sympathetic, and shows his very genuine desire to understand and sympathize before criticizing. In fact, one of the interesting features of *The Rebel* is the struggle which is occasionally visible between Camus as a hostile critic for moral motives, and Camus as a sympathetic critic for aesthetic or emotional reasons. It is unfortunate that, in general, the hostile and moral critic dominates. As Malraux remarked: 'It is not passion which destroys a work of art, but the desire to prove something.' Camus had enabled his passion to express itself in the prose of *The Myth of Sisyphus*; he had refused to allow it to appear in *The Rebel* until the last rhetorical passage. This, with its unfortunate pomposity, showed how far he had failed to repeat the success of *The Myth of Sisyphus*. Then he had written, of the strange joy which comes over Sisyphus as he realizes his fate, that 'in the world suddenly returned to its silence, the thousand little enraptured voices of the earth come into life'. In *The Rebel* he proclaims with a certain self-importance: 'We shall choose Ithaca, the faithful earth, audacious and frugal thought, the generosity of the man who knows.' The lyricism of *The Myth of Sisyphus* is genuine, that of *The Rebel* seems forced and is an attempt to reintroduce feeling into a world from which an excess of logic has banished it.

The Rebel is, nevertheless, to be admired both for its intentions and for its basic idea. It is because, in the twentieth century, ideology has become what Camus most detests—a justification of killing and a large-scale user of capital punishment—that he is so obsessed with its importance. It is because politics in his own time have been so dominated by the question of murder that he assumes that the real problem is the moral basis of the right to kill. The twentieth century has witnessed a disregard for the sanctity of the individual unprecedented in civilized society, and Camus is most admirable in his insistence upon facing this problem. His anti-communism is completely disinterested and is inspired by the highest motives—respect for the individual and horror at the way in which he is sacrificed to preconceived theories and ideas. It is true that he is, in *The Rebel*, risking the danger of merely preaching to the converted, and that it is unlikely that his arguments will ever have any effect upon the ruthlessness of contemporary politicians. However, in assuming, by the very act of writing this book, that men may still in their political actions be influenced by reason and moderation, Camus is keeping alive the much needed tradition of liberalism. He does so in a way which is particularly useful in the history of European thought. Too long the tradition and idea of revolt among European intellectuals have been associated with violence, excess, nihilism, hatred and provocation of God, and indifference to man. Camus, like George Orwell, has the feelings of the common man and the mind of an intellectual. He sees revolt as it really is for the ordinary person—a protest against suffering and injustice and not an attempt radically to transform the nature of the world. He points out that the right way to protest against the injustice, the cruelty and the disorder of the world is to try to realize those specifically human qualities of order, mercy and justice. It is a truism to insist upon this, but a truism which it has become necessary to state in the peculiar tradition of revolt such as Camus found it in the intellectual atmosphere of his time. The extent to which this tradition of revolt is considered important will, inevitably, determine the importance attributed to *The Rebel* as a representation of the lot of modern man.

It is obvious that part of the tradition which Camus attacks is rather esoteric—the influence of Sade, Rimbaud, Lautréamont, the Russian nihilists is relatively small. That of Hegel and Marx, while enormous, is certainly not as exclusive as Camus would maintain. While justification can be found in the work of Hegel for almost any political idea, and while Marx declared that no one could fully understand his system without having first of all understood the whole of the *Logic* of Hegel, the development of communism into a bloody and ruthless dictatorship cannot be considered as primarily a result of their philosophy. All tyrannies like to drape themselves in a philosophy, and in the country where they are established this philosophy is inferior in importance to their real political, military and economic power. It is when they are attempting to infiltrate into other countries that their philosophies are used, especially if the country under attack is philosophical in temperament. This is certainly the case of mid-twentieth-century France, with its large number of communist and fellow-travelling intellectuals, and it was to them that Camus's book was primarily addressed. It is natural, therefore, that its appeal should be limited for an outside audience. Even in France itself, however, its intellectual influence over the fellow travellers is likely to be very much less than the military suppression of the Hungarian revolt.

The relative failure of *The Rebel*, combined with the indisputable inferiority as plays of *State of Siege* and *The Just* to *Caligula* and *Cross-Purpose*, seems to underline the truth of Gide's remark that '*C'est avec de bons sentiments qu'on fait de la mauvaise littérature*'. It is true that *Cross-Purpose* did not have a great deal of success when it was produced in Paris in 1944, and it ran for only forty performances. Critics insisted upon the improbable melodrama of the plot—it was strange, they said, that no one had ever noticed the disappearance of former travellers—and they also pointed out that the play was insufficient as proof of the absurd since all the conditions had been carefully planned to demonstrate absurdity from the very beginning. Criticisms like this are valid only to the extent to which *Cross-Purpose* is considered as a semi-realistic play and not as a myth. The fatality which it expresses is as improbable as that of *Oedipus Rex*, and almost as overwhelming. The economy of construction, the terseness of the dialogue and the simplicity of the action all fit the expression of the dour, pessimistic theme. The hesitating conversation between Jan and his sister, the atmosphere of fatality which dominates their meeting, the final brutal shock of the discovery of the truth amply compensate for the improbable melodrama of the actual intrigue. It contains a cry of absolute misery and despair which shows the depths of pessimism to which Camus can descend. At the end of the play, the mother is forced into a recantation of her complete lack of moral principles in a most ironically tragic speech. 'This proves that, in a world in which everything can be denied, there are undeniable forces, and that on this earth where nothing is assured, we have our certainties. The love of a mother for her son is now my certainty.' It is the existence of the closest human relationships which is menaced by the absurd—hence the choice of the death of Meursault's mother in order to symbolize his indifference—and the mother in *Cross-Purpose* makes the terrible discovery that 'this world in itself is not reasonable, and I have every right to say so, for I have tasted all it has to offer, from creation to destruction'.

The fact that *Cross-Purpose* was less successful as a play than *Caligula* is explained by the static nature of the plot, the lack of probability of the story, and its atmosphere of unrelieved, monotonous gloom. *Caligula* combines the exuberance of *Ubu Roi*—with which several critics compared it—with the pathetic beauty of the Persian legend of Prince Siddharta leaving his father's house on his discovery of human sorrow. There is a carefully planned correspondence between the sudden violent changes of scene and action and Caligula's unpredictable fits of temperament. The rhetoric of certain scenes suits Caligula's own histrionic character, while in others the quiet, subdued, prosaic language—as in the conversation between Caligula and Hélicon—expresses the seriousness of Caligula's anguish. His discovery of 'a completely simple, completely clear truth, and a rather stupid one, but one which it is difficult to discover and heavy to bear ... men die and they are not happy', is the clearest proof of the utter lack of harmony between man and the world, and of the irredeemable nature of the absurd. Caligula is brother to Meursault, and the reactions of both characters towards the same discovery—the reality of death—are both equally convincing. *Caligula*, written in 1938, but possibly altered before being first staged in 1944, has all the qualities of a young man's play—exuberance, freshness, vitality and purity. It strangely foreshadowed the Europe of the early 1940's, with its victory of mad emperors apparently devoted to demonstrating the world's absurdity. The fact that this foreshadowing was unconscious adds to, rather than detracts from, the value of the play as a description of the lot of man at a particular moment of history. It is perhaps because *Cross-Purpose* was written in the winter of 1943, almost with the deliberate aim of expressing the futile tragedy of modern life, that it is inferior to *Caligula*. Camus's work is often the acutest expression of modern sensibility when it is the result of purely personal feelings and experience.

State of Siege and *The Just*, both of which are deliberately contemporary plays, seem to prove this statement by their failure. Rarely has a play by an important modern author, produced by one of France's leading actor-managers, had such a disastrous critical reception as *State of Siege*. Bernard Simiot expressed the general reaction when he wrote that it was 'a spectacle that is often boring, wordy and grandiloquent, interspersed with bad revue scenes or incomprehensible ballets, animated by symbolic characters in whose suffering or loves it is extremely difficult to take any interest'. The principal reason for this failure lies in Camus's deliberate intention of equating the plague with totalitarianism, which leads him to make it far too conscious of its own nature. Whatever Camus may say, modern totalitarianism does not deliberately and consciously set out to destroy human happiness, but merely sacrifices it to a so-called general good. Had the plague in *State of Siege*—as it had in *The Plague*—imposed quarantine, separation, and bureaucratic regulations because they were 'good for' the inhabitants of Cadiz, then the play would have been infinitely more convincing. Camus made the plague too exuberantly boastful in the proclamation of its aims. In fact, these are not the conscious aims of totalitarianism and cannot be convincingly represented as such. They are an inevitable part of its nature, but are never openly formulated as its ends. Camus oversimplified both ideas and characters in *State of Siege*, and it is far more easy to sympathize with Caligula than with Diégo and Maria.

The Just shares with *Caligula* the largest number of performances of any play so far written by Camus. Both ran for over four hundred performances, and, in the case of *The Just*, this is certainly a tribute to the patience of the Parisian theatre audience. It is a most sincere and idealistic play, but also rather verbose, rhetorical and naïve. The whole question of the play is the assassination of the Grand Duke, which does not seem likely to make any particular contribution to the coming of the revolution. Camus is concerned only with pointing a moral, and showing how far the communists of 1950 have fallen from the idealists of 1905. His presentation of the problems of revolutionary action is greatly inferior to that of Sartre or Malraux, largely because he is only capable of showing one aspect of these problems. One has only to compare *The Just* with *Les Mains Sales* to see how oversimplified Camus's ideas are. It is curious that since *The Just*, Camus has turned to the adaptation of other people's plays—Calderón de la Barca, *La Devoción à la Crux;* Pierre de Larivey, *Les Esprits;* Tino Buzatti, *Un caso clinico—*

and, in 1956, Faulkner's novel, *Requiem for a Nun*. He describes the theatre as his hobby, and is fascinated by it because, as he says, it is the only artistic activity in which the team spirit is more important than the individual. It is possible that, with a more thorough knowledge of stagecraft and what can be expressed on the stage, he will be able in the future to use the theatre convincingly to express his own ideas.

The principal criticism of Camus's journalistic writing is that there is not enough of it. This is because he is first and foremost a moralist, and the potentialities of morality are soon exhausted in this medium. His two main excursions into journalism are the *Letters to a German Friend* and *Neither Victims nor Executioners*, and both of these are more in the nature of pamphlets of political morality than of ordinary journalism. The *Letters to a German Friend* are typical of the literature produced in France by the German occupation. Instead of imitating the fiercely chauvinistic pamphlets written by Barrès, Déroulède and Claudel during the first world war, French writers between 1940 and 1945 used the problems of the occupation and the Resistance movement in order to underline the basic tragedy of the human condition. It is this fact which ensures for the *Letters to a German Friend* a greater permanent appeal than is possessed by any patriotic literature written between 1914 and 1918. The problems treated by Camus are those of an idealist in wartime—'we wanted only to love our country in justice as well as in truth and hope'—as well as the general question of the whole foundation of morality in the modern age. In the last letter Camus goes beyond the immediate question of the attitude towards the German invader, and writes a general profession of humanist faith. One of his main achievements, as a writer on contemporary problems, has been to restate these principles in a new and pessimistic context. 'You have chosen injustice, you have taken the side of the gods. Your logic was only apparent. I have chosen justice, on the contrary, to remain faithful to the earth. I still think that the world has no general significance. But I know that something in it has meaning, and that is man, because he is the only being to demand that he should have one.' It may be that this is rhetoric rather than factual journalism, but insofar as the problem of our time is a problem of recreating values, Camus provides a convincing and moving reply to it.

Neither Victims nor Executioners is an extremely effective piece of writing, from its opening sentence onwards: 'The seventeenth century was the century of mathematics, the eighteenth that of physics and the nineteenth that of biology. Our century is the century of fear.' This is certainly an accurate description of the fate of modern man, though not one which it requires a great deal of originality to make. Camus writes an impassioned protest against murder and intolerance used as political weapons, and denounces the belief in abstract and all-embracing systems as the cause for their universal use in the twentieth century. It is tempting to reply: 'Yes, we know, but we can do nothing about it. This is what liberals have been saying for centuries, but things get worse rather than better while we protest.' It is as much in the context of revolt as in that of the absurd that the morality of *The Myth of Sisyphus* is needed. The liberal needs to repeat over and over again—as Camus does in his journalism—that tolerance and understanding are the *sine qua non* of any satisfactory political attitude, and hope that one day the stone will remain on the top of the hill. The other possible form of journalistic activity, that pursued by Sartre in *Les Temps Modernes*—the denunciation of injustice everywhere, but particularly in America and the West—is possibly to be preferred to that of Camus. In fact, it is one of the main criticisms that a foreign, and particularly an English reader is tempted to make of both Camus's journalism and his philosophical writings: that in an age where the most important questions are those of social organization, he should be concerned too much with abstract philosophy. It is difficult to agree with the numerous French critics who say that Camus's work fully reflects the problems of our age *because* it is highly metaphysical. The principal problem of our century is not to find out which values need to be pursued, for everyone agrees that tolerance and social justice are the only possible criteria by which a society can be judged, but to find ways and means of realizing these values. Camus's journalism makes little or no contribution to this problem. It is a sincere and convincing account of his own feelings, but little more. The fact that he has now decided to give up journalism—which is not the same thing as refusing to take sides on important political issues—seems to indicate that like his own character, Jonah, he feels more in solidarity with his time when he is working alone as a creative artist than when he is trying to grapple face to face with its problems.

*way to realizing values.

There is no doubt that, artistically speaking, Camus's lyrical essays and his 'novels' are the best part of his work. *The Outsider*, *The Plague* and *The Fall* all have certain qualities in common, which single them out as masterpieces of their kind. All keep the reader's attention from beginning to end. The objections which the reader may feel towards the ideas the novels express in no way interfere with his pleasure in reading them. All tell a story and tell it well. Each of them is a carefully planned work of art, in which Camus holds the balance between a particular style demanded by the subject and his own personal, lyrical way of writing. Each of them is at one and the same time a realistic story and a myth, something for the reader and something for the critic. Each combines the expression of part of Camus's personal experience with the description of an aspect of man's fate in the twentieth century.

It is interesting to note that when *The Outsider* was first published, a few months before *The Myth of Sisyphus*, two of the critics who reviewed it saw it as a naturalistic piece of writing, and did not understand its meaning until they had read Camus's essay. This is a tribute to Camus's powers as a story-teller rather than a criticism of his ability to express a philosophical idea in the medium of fiction. Meursault is primarily a clerk working in Algiers, who loses his mother, takes a mistress, becomes involved in an unsavoury affair which is not his concern, shoots a man by accident and is condemned to death. It was not only because Camus used Hemingway's technique of short, disconnected sentences to express the notion of the absurd that *The Outsider* was so frequently compared to an American novel. Meursault seemed very near to the Blondy Niles of Caldwell's *Poor Fool*, the translation of which, in 1945, was enthusiastically received by French critics. He was, like the Lemmy of *Of Mice and Men*, the innocent caught up and killed by a wicked world. Although this impression is one which illustrates the different ways in which *The Outsider* can be appreciated, it is one which soon disappears on a closer reading of the novel. Meursault is not the moron, very like a 'dumb ox', whom Wyndham Lewis considered him to be, but the representative of a valid and defensible attitude towards life. The deliberate simplicity of Camus's style of narration does not only show the atomistic view of the universe as it appears to the absurd man. It also serves to underline the stupidity of many of society's assumptions, in exactly the same way as does a similar technique in *Candide* or *Les Lettres Persanes*. At the same time, it presents the hero of the story as a man whose attitude is justified and reasonable.

There are few more efficient ways of discrediting an established institution than pretending, in the description which one gives of it, to understand neither its nature nor its function. This is precisely what Camus is doing in *The Outsider*. His intentions can best be judged by comparing the novel to Kafka's *The Trial*. In 1945, Etiemble described both books as exact expressions of the human condition in their treatment of the same incomprehensible condemnation which hung over modern man. Camus's attitude, however, is vastly different from that of Kafka. In *The Trial*, Joseph K does not question the validity of the charges laid against him. Nowhere in the novel is he allowed to adopt a critical and cynical attitude towards the judges. Although Meursault does not struggle against his fate, and does little to protect himself, this is not because he does not understand what is happening. He is accused, but he does not accept his guilt. If he shows little inclination to fight against his condemnation, it is because this would involve the loss of his honesty and integrity, and his acceptance, if only temporarily, of society's conventions. Meursault, condemned partly for his intransigent honesty, does not fail in his turn to judge society. The reader, obliged by Camus's technique to adopt Meursault's point of view, sympathizes with him and not with society. Society is lifeless and mechanistic, concerned only with appearances, and unable to understand anything which does not fit in with its preconceived notions of behaviour. It condemns Meursault to death because he will not tell lies about how he felt on the day of his mother's funeral, not because he killed the Arab. It is made quite clear that had he been prepared to show remorse and act the part of the dutiful son and repentant criminal, he would have only been sent to prison for a few years, and might even have escaped scot-free. In saying of him that he is 'the only kind of Christ whom we deserve', Camus is insisting not only upon Meursault's innocence but also upon his virtue. At the same time as Camus's use of Hemingway's technique helps him to satirize society, his own instinctively lyrical style expresses not only what Meursault has to live for, but also the real reasons for his shooting the Arab.

Meursault's awareness of the colours, lights and sensations of the external world is so acute as to recall at times a mystical experience. Objects exist for him in their absolute newness as they exist for the illuminate. He delights in existence such as he finds it, and each detail is for him infinitely important. This importance of physical existence is, in *The Outsider*, part of the expression of the absurdity of the world. When no emotions or ideas have any significance, physical events alone are capable of influencing a man and making him act. It is not hatred, envy, greed, revenge or honour which makes Meursault kill the Arab, but simply the effect of the sun. This is the only explanation which he can give of his act, and since he is not very good at expressing himself, it is one which society cannot understand or accept. The reader, however, is made to see the extreme importance of physical objects by the vividness of the language used, and by the multiplicity of images which occur in the description of the murder of the Arab. When Meursault's act comes upon him—he does not say that he pulled the trigger, only that 'the trigger gave way'—sun and sea are strongly personified as living creatures exercising an overwhelming influence upon him. The sun strikes as with cymbals on his forehead and the sea engulfs him in its hot thick breath. He is entirely possessed by the forces of nature and is passive under their influence. In an absurd world, where sensations and objects are all-important, they are also ambivalent. In the second half of the book, Meursault's most trivial acts form crushing evidence against him. The sea and the sun, the objects of his only enthusiasm, impel him to commit the crime for which he will be executed. In *The Outsider*, one half of Camus's technique enables him to express the 'weariness tinged with amazement' which is Meursault's attitude towards life, at the same time as his own highly poetical, personal style gives conviction to the idea that only physical existence matters or can influence action in an absurd world. Technique and metaphysics are, in *The Outsider*, completely merged, one supporting and reinforcing the other. The novel, from this point of view, has more unity than *The Plague*, and even the protest against capital punishment in the second part of the book fits into its general theme of the immense value of the individual physical life.

Camus said that *The Outsider* was an exercise in objectivity, the impersonal working out of the logical results of the philosophy of the absurd. *The Plague*, on the other hand, he said, was a personal confession. While one may find it difficult to believe that there was at the time of writing no identification between Camus and Meursault, *The Outsider* is so controlled a work of art that everything in it has a completely independent existence of its own. The same thing can be said of *The Plague*, where Camus's use of a technique which he deliberately assumes for a particular purpose also enables him to create a classical work of art. It is evident that it was from the feeling of separation that Camus suffered most during the Occupation, and it is to the analysis of separation that he devotes much of *The Plague*. He does not, however, do so in a personal style which would directly express his own private emotions. In the description of separation his tone is at its most ironic and most controlled, and the effect which it obtains is consequently greater. One of the best known passages of the novel treats of this feeling and is an excellent example of Camus's style.

'*Une des conséquences les plus remarquables de la fermeture des portes fut, en effet, la soudaine séparation où furent placés des êtres qui n'y étaient point préparés. Des mères et des enfants, des époux, des amants qui avaient cru procéder quelques jours auparavant à une séparation temporaire, qui s'étaient embrassés sur le quai de notre gare avec deux ou trois recommandations, certains de se revoir quelques jours ou quelques semaines plus tard, enfoncés dans la stupide confiance humaine, à peine distraits par ce départ de leurs préoccupations habituelles, se virent d'un seul coup éloignés sans recours, empêchés de se rejoindre ou de communiquer. Car la fermeture s'était faite quelques heures avant que l'arrêt préfectoral fut publié, et, naturellement, il était impossible de prendre en considération des cas particuliers.*'

('One of the most noteworthy results of the closing of the city gates was, in fact, the sudden separation which it imposed upon people who were not prepared for it. Mothers and children, married couples, lovers, who had thought a few days previously that they would be separated only for a short time, who had kissed good-bye on the station platform with one or two pieces of advice, certain that they would meet again a few days or a few weeks later, sunk in stupid human confidence, their thoughts scarcely taken away by this departure from their everyday preoccupations, suddenly found themselves irretrievably separated, prevented from meeting or communicating with one another. For the gates had been shut a few hours before the prefectoral decision was made public, and it was naturally impossible to take individual cases into consideration.')

The constant understatement in the descriptive style of *The Plague*, the precise use of administrative terms and official language, the deliberate banality of the words, are essential elements in the final effect which the chronicle makes. The impersonal mode of narration allows the author to act on the reader's sensitivity without revealing his own, to create emotion in the reader's mind by forcing him to project his own feelings onto the extraordinary events so calmly described. The irony of Camus's style is the most important factor in bringing out the full horror of the situation, and his use of understatement plays an essential rôle in establishing the relationship between reality and allegory. His aim is to equate plague with the bureaucratic tyranny of a modern dictatorship, and he does it by describing plague as manifesting itself in the same way and having the very same effects as bureaucracy.

A good example of this is in his evocation of the monotony of the period of plague.

'*Dans le souvenir de ceux qui les ont vécues, les journées terribles de la peste n'apparaissent pas comme de grandes flammes interminables et cruelles, mais plutôt comme un immense piétinement qui écrasait tout sur son passage.*'

('In the memory of those who lived through them, the terrible days of the plague do not seem like great, cruel, interminable flames, but rather like an endless movement of feet which crushed everything it passed over.')

Here his words apply exactly both to the period of German occupation and to the effect which a plague would have upon a modern city. The essential services would be maintained, as they were maintained in occupied France. The primitive terror of plague would bring a reinforcement in the discipline of the day-to-day government of the city. The horror of pestilence would be hidden for the most part under a monotonous administration and reveal itself only suddenly and in unexpected places—at the

theatre, where an actor is stricken down in the middle of his
rôle, in a restaurant where a diner is suddenly taken ill. In
earlier plagues, in more primitive times, the carts went round the
streets to collect the dead, whose bodies were heaped in confusion one upon another. In Oran, the dead are scientifically
collected, disinfected, loaded into trams and carried by night to
the pits of quicklime. The excellence of Camus's description lies
precisely in the contrast which he maintains between the
physical, primitive horror of the plague, and the quiet, scientific
administration of the modern city, between the awfulness of the
events and the everyday places where they occur. His skill in
alternating them—evident in the description of the incident at
the theatre and of the sudden shock when Rieux's foot squelches
upon the dead rat in the middle of his landing—is combined
with an extremely effective style. When Rieux discovers the rat
on his landing, the incident is described as '*insolite*'. Camus's
deliberate refusal to use any other but the most precise and
simple words in most of the descriptive passages enables him to
throw into high relief those scenes to which he wishes to attach
a special significance.

The two most important scenes, from this point of view, are
the death of judge Othon's son and Tarrou's confession. Like
the murder of the Arab in *The Outsider*, the death of the child is
one of the most important incidents in *The Plague*, and like the
shooting of the Arab it is described in an intensely poetic
passage.

'*Il resta creusé ainsi pendant de longues secondes, secoué de
frissons et de tremblements convulsifs, comme si sa frêle
carcasse pliait sous le vent furieux de la peste et craquait sous
les souffles répétés de la fièvre. La bourrasque passée, il se
détendit un peu, la fièvre sembla se retirer et l'abandonner,
haletant, sur une grève humide et empoisonnée où le repos
ressemblait déjà à la mort.*'

('The child remained bent over for long moments, quivering
and shuddering in long trembling fits, as if his frail body were
bending beneath the furious wind of the plague and cracking
beneath the repeated gusts of fever. The squall ceased, he
relaxed a little, the fever seemed to withdraw and leave him,
panting, on a damp and poisoned bank where rest was
already like death.')

Similarly, when Rieux and Tarrou confirm their friendship by a symbolic bathe together, the sea is described with a comparable wealth of poetic imagery—*'épaisse comme du velours, souple et lisse comme une bête'*, a beast whose calm breathing *'faisait naître et disparaître des reflets huileux à la surface des eaux'*. It is when Camus uses phrases such as these, or when he describes the effect of sun and heat in North Africa—

'A certaines heures, la campagne est noire de soleil. Les yeux tentent vainement de saisir autre chose que des gouttes de lumière qui tremblent au bord des cils.'

('At certain times of day, the countryside is black with sunlight. The eyes strive in vain to hold on to anything but the drops of light which tremble on the eyelashes.')

—that he is writing most naturally and makes his most genuine appeal. It is, however, a measure of his achievement that he has, in *The Plague* and in *The Outsider*—as well as in *The Fall*—successfully adopted a completely different style because he felt that the subjects demanded a particular treatment. The importance which Camus has had, for the young Frenchman of his generation, as a philosopher and moralist, is always, in the final analysis, based upon his excellence as a writer of French, and it is in a way regrettable that, in general, far more consideration should have been given to him as a thinker than as an artist.

This is probably because Camus has always been so successful as an artist that there has not been a great deal that one could say about him in this respect, whereas many of his ideas are not only extremely stimulating to discuss, but are also quite easy to criticize. This is particularly so in *The Fall*, where the ambiguity of what the book says easily distracts attention from the question of how it says it. Artistically, *The Fall* is first and foremost a study in the spirit of place. In *The Plague* and *The Outsider*, the clear light of North Africa formed an appropriate background for the discussion of definite questions—life and death, solitude or communion, good and evil, suffering and happiness. The sun dominates the whole of the action in *The Outsider*, obsessing Meursault at his mother's funeral, giving him pleasure when he is with Maria, making him kill the Arab, reminding him at his trial that a year has passed since his adventure first started, and pouring in through the windows of the court-room. In the same way, rain and mist determine the psychological atmosphere of *The Fall*, casting a strange light in which guilt and innocence, pride and humility, irony and deadly seriousness, are impossible to identify and distinguish one from the other. At Amsterdam, the sea is no longer shimmering under the powerful sun, but 'steaming like a laundry', stretching without limits around Clamence and his listener as they sail across the Zuydersee. Camus combines with his own skill in describing places a talent almost equal to that of Sartre for satirizing hypocrisy and bad faith. Clamence speaks as one would expect one of the '*salauds*' in the municipal art-gallery at Bouville to speak, if once he had attained sufficient self-consciousness to be aware of himself. The myth which Camus is expressing in *The Fall* is almost as widespread as those which he had expressed in *The Outsider* and *The Plague*. In concentrating attention upon the problems of human duplicity and dishonesty, Camus is continuing in the medium of the novel that examination of man's fate in the twentieth century which he had already expressed in the myth of the outsider in his first novel, and in the myth of imprisonment and impotence in *The Plague*.

Camus's treatment of the outsider myth is one of the most interesting in modern literature. There are many parallels to Meursault—Sartre's Roquentin, Anouilh's Antigone, Gide's '*immoraliste*', Malraux's Garine—who all express the same refusal of bourgeois society and, implicitly, demand that it should be re-established on a new code of values. Meursault is the purest example of the type. His refusal is not based upon an ethic of self-development as is Michel's, on idealistic purity as is Antigone's, on Nietzschean self-assertion like Garine's or on violent hatred like Roquentin's, but simply on a calm recognition of the emptiness of human pretence. His lack of illusions is absolute. When his lawyer asks him if he suffered on the day of his mother's funeral—a question which Meursault would have found very embarrassing to have to ask someone else—he replies frankly: 'Certainly I loved Mother, but that didn't mean anything. All normal people had more or less wished for the death of their loved ones.' At the same time as he is incapable of masking the truth of the human condition, he most definitely has something to live for. In his cell, he discovers that a man need only have lived through one day to have sufficient memories to last him in captivity for the rest of his life. When the chaplain asks him to think of all the criminals who, in the condemned cell, have seen the Divine Face appear in its walls, Meursault replies that, in truth, he had looked for a face in them. 'But this face had the colour of the sun and the flame of desire. It was the face of Marie.' It is the fact that Meursault really has something to live for—unlike Antigone, Roquentin and Garine, who live only in their ideas and in their refusal—which distinguishes him from them. The authenticity of Camus's love of life, and his rigorous honesty make his conversion to humanism in *The Plague* more genuine and more interesting. *The Plague* is all the more moving as an expression of the impotence of men of good will in the modern world because of the evident sincerity of Camus's attitude. When Rieux stands 'on the bank, empty-handed, his heart torn with anguish, once again helpless and without weapons against the disaster', and watches Tarrou die, he foreshadows the impotence of the free world to do anything at all to save Hungary in 1956. It is the recognition of the limits of the moral attitude described in *The Plague* which is the clearest proof of Camus's intellectual honesty. He does not say that what Rieux does is perfect, but simply that it is all that he possibly can do without betraying his own ideals. One may feel that these ideals are of such a nature that they prevent all effective action, but still admire the consistency of Camus's attitude. This consistency is not in any way impaired by the ambiguity of *The Fall*. To admit that man is cruel, hypocritical and self-centred does not imply that one renounces all attempts to establish a humanistic ethic. Camus has faced this problem of man's imperfection in *The Fall*, and indicated one of the disastrous results which can follow the negation of the idea of man's *relative* innocence on which he has always insisted, and which he has tried to establish for himself. *The Fall* unmasks a 'leap' in the same way as did *The Myth of Sisyphus* and *The Rebel*. In it, Camus remains faithful to the limited nature of all human activity. No attitude, he has always maintained, is so free from error as to require our complete allegiance. It may be that the scepticism towards established religious, political or literary groupings which is advocated in all Camus's works will, in the long run, be most likely to achieve his dearest aim—the reduction of the sum total of human suffering. Originally, his work was to be a hymn of praise to Creation, and an expression of the delights and happiness of life. He wanted, as he said in 1949, to be able to write as Mozart composed music. This is an ambition which he still has, but one which he knows cannot be realized by turning his back upon the human tragedy. It is from Camus's awareness of this tragedy, coupled with his integrity both as a thinker and as an artist, that we can confidently expect many more admirable works of art from one of the greatest humanists of our day.

CAMUS AND CAPITAL PUNISHMENT
A SUPPLEMENTARY NOTE

IN June and July 1957 Camus published, in the *Nouvelle Nouvelle Revue Française*, an essay entitled *Réflexions sur la Guillotine*, shortly to appear in a work on capital punishment of which he is joint author with Arthur Koestler.[1] Abhorrence for capital punishment is one of the main—one might almost say *the* main—theme of Camus's work. It occurs in his first essays, in *The Outsider* and in *The Myth of Sisyphus* ('the opposite of a man who commits suicide is a man condemned to death'), is central to the message of *The Plague*, and dominates the whole of Camus's political thinking. This is the first time, however, that he has put forward a reasoned argument against the death penalty.

He begins by relating one of the few incidents he knows concerning his father, who was killed in the battle of the Marne in 1914. His father had one day decided to go and witness the execution of a man who had murdered a family of small-holders, and of whom he had declared, in company with many others, that 'the guillotine was too good for him'. He never described what happened at the execution. Camus's mother simply related that he tore into the house, his face stricken with horror, lay down on his bed and was violently sick. 'He had just discovered,' writes Camus, 'the reality which lay behind the high-sounding phrases which disguised it.'

Clearly this incident—or rather his mother's description of it —made a deep impression upon Camus, and certainly determined his initial emotional opposition to the death penalty, in the same way as his recovery from tuberculosis had intensified his awareness of physical life. The rest of the essay, however, is without any open expression of the emotion which he has obvious difficulty in containing. Camus examines the various arguments put forward in favour of capital punishment. If it is intended to frighten potential murderers, why then does the execution take place in private, and why is it described—in

[1] *Réflexions sur la Peine de Mort*. Camus and Koestler.

France at any rate—in such euphemistic and neutral terms? If society really believed what it said, then executions, if not public, would at least be fully described in the press. In fact, the last time that this happened in France—in 1939—*Paris-Soir* was reproved by the government for encouraging the sadistic tendencies of its readers. Camus gives, by quotations from medical witnesses, details of the act of execution by guillotine which are certainly enough to deter anyone likely to stop and think before killing. He opens his argument in the same way as does Tarrou in *The Plague*, who describes how a firing squad stands barely two yards away from the victim and how the bullets make a hole in his chest as big as a man's fist. Now, however, Camus does not limit himself to evoking the physical horror of execution.

Capital punishment does not, in fact, deter, he continues, and uses the examples and statistics taken from Koestler and the report of the British Royal Commission to show that an increase in the number of murders does not follow the abolition of the death penalty. It is uncertain, he argues, that capital punishment does deter would-be murderers—at least, it can never be *proved* that it does—whereas it is absolutely certain that it does kill men. Indeed, far from deterring murderers—which it *may* do—capital punishment exercises so powerful an influence upon certain minds that the number of applicants for the post of executioner by far exceeds the vacancies. It is likely, Camus points out, that unsuccessful candidates may satisfy their ambitions elsewhere.

Capital punishment, he continues, is merely the expression of vengeance by a society which does not believe sufficiently in their deterrent capacity to make executions public. But, for vengeance to be justified, the avenger must be innocent, and society is not innocent of the crimes which its members commit. This is particularly so in France, where bad housing and alcoholism—the first due to state inertia, the second, at least in part, to state subsidy—contribute to an estimated 60 per cent of crimes of violence. It cannot claim the absolute innocence which would alone give it the right to kill. Neither, at present, has the state the religious or metaphysical right to execute criminals. The Catholic Church justifies capital punishment by the argument that it is not a final and absolute judgment. The soul is immortal and God the final judge. Human justice is not regarded as definitive and its verdict is not final. In a society which fully accepted Christian theology, this idea—however contrary it may be, Camus remarks, to the teaching of Christ—could provide the justification for execution. But our own society no longer has this absolute religious belief. The judge who pronounces sentence may be an atheist or an agnostic who, believing only in the existence of this life, is thereby giving a definite and irredeemable verdict. He pronounces the criminal absolutely and irretrievably guilty, depriving him of any chance of improving or reforming himself, or attempting—however inadequately— to put right the wrong he has done. By the standards of a non-religious society—our own—capital punishment is definitive in an abstract moral sense. It is also definitive in a very practical way.

In Belgium, it was discovered that a man had been unjustly executed, and as a result of that discovery, Belgium abolished the death penalty. In France, England and America there are cases where a similar irretrievable mistake is suspected. Society has no right to kill unless it is absolutely certain, first of all, that it has a religious or metaphysical right to do so, and that there is no possible doubt in each particular case that there is no error of legal judgment. Neither of these two conditions, given the essentially limited nature of human knowledge—in both general, philosophical matters, and in the practical details of evidence— can ever be realized.

It is here that this essay on the death penalty most closely follows the ideas which Camus has expressed in his other works. Essential to his idea of revolt, and to the humanism which he draws from it, is the acceptance of limits and the recognition of human fallibility. Because we can never be certain that we are completely right, we can never be justified in performing actions as irretrievable and absolute as taking a man's life away from him. Our fallibility does not mean that we have no right to act or to punish—Camus suggests life imprisonment as an alternative to capital punishment—but it does imply that we should always hesitate before acting as if we were completely right.

The end of the essay takes us fully into the field which Camus has made his own speciality—the attack against European nihilism and against the worship of the state. What is needed to-day, and needed urgently, Camus argues, is protection for the individual against the enormously increased danger that he may one day be executed by the state for political reasons. Such a possibility would have seemed laughable—in Western Europe at least—at the beginning of this century, but is uncomfortably likely to-day. Without the right of the state to execute criminals, both political and ordinary, modern history—indeed all history —would be a more bearable spectacle. Camus proposes that the first article of the code of the United Europe which will to-morrow, he says, be a reality, should be the formal abolition of the death penalty.

That Camus should at the present moment of French history (July 1957), with almost open warfare raging in his native Algeria, put all his considerable moral authority in an appeal for the abolition of capital punishment, raises an interesting question regarding *la littérature engagée*. Should the writer devote himself to specifically political questions—like the Algerian war, the Suez crisis or the Hungarian revolt—or should he be concerned with the more general moral questions which Camus discusses in this essay? For Sartre, the limited political questions are the more important. In a bitterly sarcastic article *Vous êtes formidables* (*Les Temps Modernes*, May 1957) he violently attacks the use of torture in Algeria, and gives publicity to a pamphlet published by the *Comité de Résistance spirituelle* which provides details of the accusations levelled against the pacifying forces. Where, asks Sartre, are the *grandes voix* which so loudly—*and with complete justification*—denounced the Russian intervention in Hungary? This seems an obvious appeal to Camus, whose moral authority is at least as great as that of Sartre. Camus, as he himself pointed out in a letter to *Encounter* in June 1957, has already made his position clear on Algeria, demanding an end of colonial practices and the setting up of a federation which would assure both Arabs and European settlers equal rights, and he is not a writer who is given to excessive repetition of his political suggestions. Nevertheless he has not, at the time of writing, joined with Sartre in protesting against this particular abuse, although his general attitude leaves no doubt that he would not hesitate to condemn it absolutely. Neither, however, did he join in October 1956 with François Mauriac, who was almost the only non-communist French writer to protest against the Anglo-French invasion of Suez. His left-wing admirers may regret this abstention, which makes him too much of an anti-communist intellectual. His attitude, how-ever, is quite consistent. He has made his opinions known on both Algeria and Hungary. His essay on capital punishment saves him from the narrow partisanship which is the danger threatening the committed writer. It is a root cause of evil whose extirpation—particularly in the form which Camus proposes of refusing the state the right to use this ultimate power for political reasons—would avoid many tragic mistakes. It is unfortunate that to hope for its abolition in all countries should appear utopian.

CHAPTER ONE

In order to avoid encumbering the text with footnote numbers, all notes and references will be given simply under the page number. The French original will be given of the passages translated into English, and in certain cases an additional commentary will be added. Except in the case of *The Fall*, where use is made of Justin O'Brien's translation, I am myself responsible for the translation into English of the passages quoted.

The following abbreviations are used in the notes:

EE. – *L'Envers et l'Endroit* (*Betwixt and Between*).
N. – *Noces* (*Nuptials*).
Et. – *L'Étranger* (*The Outsider*).
MS. – *Le Mythe de Sisyphe* (*The Myth of Sisyphus*).
RR. – *La Remarque sur la Révolte* (*A Note on Revolt*).
C. – *Caligula*.
M. – *Le Malentendu* (*Cross-Purpose*).
L. – *Lettres à un ami allemand* (*Letters to a German Friend*).
ES. – *L'État de Siège* (*State of Siege*).
J. – *Les Justes* (*The Just*).
HR. – *L'Homme révolté* (*The Rebel*).
P. – *La Peste* (*The Plague*).

Except in the case of *L'Envers et l'Endroit*, where the page references are to the original Charlot edition (Algiers 1936), all references are to the standard Gallimard edition of Camus's works. A bibliography is given at the end of these notes, and wherever possible the date and publisher of the English translation is given. Only Camus's main works, however, have so far been translated into English.

p. 2. Et. p. 89. '*Et c'était comme quatre coups brefs que je frappais sur la porte du malheur.*'

Et. pp. 171-172. This most curious ending to the novel is possibly best explained by Camus's remark that Meursault was 'the only kind of Christ we deserve'—who, therefore, conscious of the fact that he is a sacrificial figure, wishes that all shall be accomplished. In an article in *Proceedings of the Modern Languages Association* (December 1956, pp. 869-887) Carl A. Vigiani suggests that Meursault represents a fusion of two mythical figures, Oedipus or the doomed

man, and Christ, the sacrificial God. Other critics have suggested that
Meursault wishes to have the feeling of living intensely at the very last
minute, which the hatred of the spectators will give him.

p. 3. Cf. MS. pp. 18 and 21. '*le caractère dérisoire de cette
habitude, le caractère insensé de cette agitation quotidienne, et
l'inutilité de la souffrance*' '*L'absurde commande-t-il la mort, il faut
donner à ce problème le pas sur les autres.*'

p. 4. MS. p. 27. '*... ce singulier état d'âme où le vide devient éloquent
... cette lassitude teintée d'étonnement.*'

MS. p. 30. '*Aucune morale ni aucun effort ne sont* à priori
*justifiables devant les sanglantes mathématiques qui ordonnent notre
condition*', i.e. in the face of inevitable death. Certain critics have
taken this phrase to refer to the particularly bloodstained history of
the twentieth century, with which Camus is more concerned in the
second part of his work. Here he is speaking of man's fate in general.
He never considers the possibility that physical death is anything but
complete annihilation. Meursault can only imagine and desire
another life in which he can remember this one.

M.S. p. 37. '*Je disais que le monde est absurde et j'allais trop vite. Ce
monde en lui-même n'est pas raisonnable, c'est tout ce qu'on en peut
dire. Mais ce qui est absurde, c'est la confrontation de cet irrationnel et
de ce désir éperdu de clarté dont l'appel résonne au plus profond de
l'homme. L'absurde dépend autant de l'homme que du monde. Il est
pour le moment leur seul lien.*'

p. 5. MS. p. 55. '*Pour un esprit absurde, la raison est vaine et il n'y a
rien au-delà de la raison.*' This attitude is one which Camus maintains
throughout the whole of his work. It is very reminiscent of Ivan
Karamazov's' Euclidean intelligence', which is incapable of accepting
replies couched in non-human, super-rational terms.

p. 6. MS. p. 76. '*Or on ne vivra pas ce destin, le sachant absurde, si on ne
fait pas tout pour maintenir devant soi cet absurde mis à jour par la
conscience. Nier l'un des termes de cette opposition, c'est lui échapper.
... Vivre, c'est faire vivre l'absurde. Au contraire d'Eurydice, l'absurde
ne meurt que lorsqu'on s'en détourne.*'

Et. p. 169. '*Rien, rien n'avait de sens et je savais pourquoi.
Lui aussi savait pourquoi. Du fond de mon avenir, pendant toute cette
vie absurde que j'avais menée, un souffle obscur remontait vers moi à
travers des années qui n'étaient pas encore venues et ce souffle égalisait
sur son passage tout ce qu'on me proposait alors dans les années pas
plus réelles que je vivais. Que m'importaient la mort des autres, l'amour
d'une mère, que m'importaient son dieu, les vies qu'on choisit puisqu'un
seul destin devait m'élire moi-même et avec moi des milliards de
privilégiés qui comme lui se disaient mes frères?*'

It has been pointed out that Meursault does not seem to achieve consciousness of the immense importance which life has for him until he is about to lose it, and that he has gone through the whole of the novel up to this point in a haze of unreality. In fact, Camus intended Meursault to be interpreted as having already gone through the experience of the absurd before the story began. The consciousness of the absurd is there all the time at the back of his mind. It is not only at the very end of the novel but all the way through that he is fully conscious that he is right to act as he does. This can be confirmed by a careful examination of the tenses used in the last passage of the novel, and also by considering the fact that Meursault does not want to change anything at all in his past life when he is about to be executed. His final protest, while also justifying him, provides a retrospective explanation of what has happened. Certain critics have thought it out of character, but there was no other way in which Camus could avoid his novel being misinterpreted.

MS. p. 80. '... *tout cela se trouve démenti de façon vertigineuse par l'absurdité d'une mort possible.*' Meursault does seem at one time to have given a certain importance to things, for he speaks on page 64 of the ambitions which he had had when he was a student, and says that when he was forced to interrupt his studies he realized that it all had no importance. The autobiographical element in his character seems quite strong here, for Camus was forced to interrupt his own studies in preparation for the *agrégation* examination in philosophy because of ill-health (attacks of tuberculosis). It may also be noted that neither Meursault nor Camus like Paris or Fernandel, whose film Meursault finds '*vraiment trop bête*' and to whom Camus refers unfavourably in an article published in 1945.

p. 7. MS. p. 84. '*la passion d'épuiser tout ce qui est donné.*'

MS. p. 96. '*Un surnuméraire aux postes est l'égal d'un conquérant si la conscience leur est commune.*'

p. 8. Et. p. 172. '... *il me restait à souhaiter qu'il y ait beaucoup de spectateurs le jour de mon exécution, et qu'ils m'accueillent avec des cris de haine.*' See note above to page 2.

Et. pp. 171-172. '*Comme si cette grande colère m'avait purgé du mal, vidé d'espoir, devant cette nuit chargée de signes et d'étoiles, je m'ouvrais pour la première fois à la tendre indifférence du monde.*'

MS. p. 168. '*Chacun des grains de cette pierre, chaque éclat minéral de cette montagne pleine de nuit, à lui seul, forme un monde. La lutte elle-même vers les sommets suffit à remplir un coeur d'homme. Il faut imaginer Sisyphe heureux.*'

MS. p. 164. '*son mépris des dieux, sa haine de la mort et sa passion pour la vie.*'

The meaning which Malraux and Sartre attach to the absurd

is different from that which Camus gives it. In *La Tentation de l'Occident* (1926) it is the conflict between man's conscious mind, which imposes morality and knowledge of good and evil, and his powerful, unconscious, non-moral emotional aspirations. In *Les Conquérants* (1928), Garine rejects society as instinctively as he rejects God. Once again, it is the conflict between instinctive and civilized man—a fact which is underlined when Garine has his greatest consciousness of the absurd in a court-room, when he is himself on trial. The parallel here between Camus and Malraux seems quite close, and it is possible that Camus is following Malraux in using Meursault's trial to underline the absurdity of much of the ordinary functioning of justice. There also seems to be a parallel between Meursault and Kyo, in *La Condition humaine*, when Meursault does not recognize his own voice when he hears it (Et. p. 116). Camus's concept of the absurd differs more from that of Sartre than from that of Malraux. For Sartre, the absurdity of existence lies in the fact that man cannot justify his own life and find his own existence necessary. For Sartre, man cannot escape from contingency and arrive at the state of pure contemplation of his own being where the '*pour-soi*' and the '*en-soi*' are one. For Sartre, 'absurd' tends to mean 'not necessary', or even (in the case of Roquentin in *La Nausée*) '*de trop*'.

p. 9.   Claude Mauriac. *La Table Ronde*, December 1951, p. 99.

'*O mon âme, n'aspire pas à la vie immortelle, mais épuise le champ du possible.*' Pindar.

p. 10. EE. p. 66. '*Je tiens au monde par tous mes gestes, aux hommes par toute ma pitié et ma reconnaissance. Entre cet envers et cet endroit du monde, je ne veux pas choisir, je n'aime pas qu'on choisisse.*'

EE. p. 20. '*Et quand est-ce que je suis plus vrai que lorsque je suis le monde?*'

EE. p. 33. '*Qu'on ne nous raconte pas d'histoires. Qu'on ne nous dise pas du condamné à mort; "il a payé sa dette à la société" mais "on va lui couper le cou". Ça n'a l'air de rien. Mais ça fait tout de même une petite différence. Et puis, il y a des gens qui préfèrent regarder leur destin dans les yeux.*'

EE. p. 30. '*Et s'il faut absolument une raison, il s'est tué parce qu'un ami lui a parlé distraitement. Ainsi, chaque fois qu'il m'a été donné d'éprouver le sens profond du monde, c'est sa simplicité qui m'a bouleversé.*'

p. 11. MS. p. 167. '*On ne découvre pas l'absurde sans être tenté d'écrire quelque manuel du bonheur.*'

N. p. 62. '*Tout ce qui exalte la vie accroît en même temps son absurdité. Dans l'été d'Algérie j'apprends qu'une seule chose est plus tragique que la souffrance, et c'est la vie d'un homme heureux. Mais ce peut être aussi le chemin d'une plus grande vie, puisque cela conduit à ne pas tricher.'*

N. p. 34. *'Que signifient les mots d'avenir, de mieux-être, de situation? Que signifie le progrès du coeur? Si je refuse obstinément tous les "plus tard" de ce monde, c'est qu'il s'agit aussi bien de ne pas renoncer à ma richesse présente.'*

p. 12. N. p. 18. *'Il me faut être nu et puis plonger dans la mer, encore tout parfumé des essences de la terre, laver celles-ci dans celle-là, et nouer sur ma peau l'étreinte pour laquelle soupirent lèvres à lèvres si longtemps la terre et la mer.'*

The use of imagery is one of the most interesting features of Camus's prose. He has various obsessions—particularly with breathing, with wind and sun, with the personification of the forces of nature. Detailed analyses of this imagery can be found in Frohock, *Image, Influence and Sensibility* (Yale French Studies, Vol. 2. No. 22. pp. 91-99) and S. John, *Image and Expression in Albert Camus* (French Studies, January 1955, pp. 42-53).

N. p. 61. *'Non qu'il faille faire la bête, mais je ne trouve pas de sens au bonheur des anges.'* An obvious reference to Pascal's *Qui veut faire l'ange, fait la bête.* There are many parallels between Camus and Pascal, although their final attitudes are completely opposed. These are:—the *'besoin d'infini'* in Pascal, corresponding to Caligula's need for the impossible, the Pascalian remark, *'Je ne puis approuver que ceux qui cherchent en gémissant'*, paralleled by the dislike for certainty and optimism which can be found in both *Caligula* and *La Peste*, the insistence on death—*'Le dernier acte est sanglant, quelque belle que soit la comédie de tout le reste'*, the Pascalian idea of man lost in a universe where nothing corresponds to his longing—*'Le silence éternel de ces vastes espaces infinis m'effraie'*, the idea of the impossibility for the human mind to attain absolute knowledge, and the final insistence upon the value of consciousness—*'L'homme n'est qu'un roseau, le plus faible de la nature, mais c'est un roseau pensant'*. In *The Unquiet Grave* (pp. 23-24), Cyril Connolly quotes a well-known passage by Pascal, and compares it to the novels of Hemingway, Sartre or Malraux—*'Qu'on s'imagine un nombre d'hommes dans les chaînes, et tous condamnés à mort, dont les uns étant chaque jour égorgés à la vue des autres, ceux qui restent voient leur propre condition dans celle de leurs semblables, et, se regardant les uns et les autres avec douleur et sans espérance, attendent leur tour. C'est l'image de la condition des hommes.'* This could equally well be taken as a description of *La Peste*, and it is possible that Camus was inspired by this passage in the extract from *La Peste* which I quote on pp. 33-4. It should, however, be noted that Pascal's final attitude is that of the existentialist 'leap' which Camus criticizes in Kierkegaard and Kafka.

He could just as easily have based *Le Mythe de Sisyphe* upon Pascal and the Book of Job.

N. p. 34. '*Il ne me plaît pas de croire que la mort ouvre sur une autre vie. Elle est pour moi une porte fermée. Je ne dis pas que c'est un pas qu'il faut franchir: mais que c'est une aventure horrible et sale. Tout ce qu'on me propose s'efforce de décharger l'homme du poids de sa propre vie. Et devant le vol lourd des grands oiseaux dans le ciel de Djémila, c'est justement un certain poids de vie que je réclame et que j'obtiens. ... J'ai trop de jeunesse en moi pour pouvoir parler de la mort. Mais il me semble que si je le devais c'est ici que je trouverais, entre l'horreur et le silence, la certitude consciente d'une mort sans espoir.*'

Sartre's *Explication de 'L'Étranger'* was first published in 1943 and reproduced in *Situations* 1 (1945).

p. 13. M. p. 28. '*On ne peut pas toujours rester un étranger, un homme a besoin de bonheur, il est vrai, mais il a aussi besoin de trouver sa définition.*' Note the two meanings of the word *étranger*—both 'outsider' and 'foreigner'.

p. 14. M. p. 56. '*cet autre pays où l'été écrase tout, où les pluies d'hiver noient les villes et où, enfin, les choses sont ce qu'elles sont.*'

M. p. 95. '*Nous sommes volés, je vous dis. À quoi bon ce grand appel vers la mer, cette alerte des âmes? Pourquoi crier vers la terre ou vers l'amour? Cela est dérisoire. Votre mari connaît maintenant la réponse, cette maison épouvantable où nous serons tous serrés les uns contre les autres.*' '*Comprenez que votre douleur ne s'égalera jamais à l'injustice qu'on fait à l'homme.*' '*Vous avez à choisir entre la stupide félicité des cailloux et ce lit gluant où nous vous attendons.*'

M. p. 59. '*la crainte qu'il n'y ait pas de réponse.*'

p. 15. M. p. 96. '*Oh, mon Dieu, je ne puis vivre dans ce désert! C'est à vous que je parlerai et je saurai trouver mes mots. ... Car c'est à vous que je m'en remets. Ayez pitié de moi, Seigneur, tournez-vous vers moi! Entendez-moi, Seigneur, donnez-moi votre main! Ayez pitié de ceux qui s'aiment et qui sont séparés.*'

It is interesting to note that the last essay in *Noces* is called *Le Désert*, and that Camus writes on p. 37 of *Le Mythe de Sisyphe*, '*Mais je veux savoir auparavant si la pensée peut vivre dans ces déserts.*' In *Le Mythe de Sisyphe*, the answer is 'Yes': in *Le Malentendu*, 'No'.

C. p. 111. '*Une vérité toute simple et toute claire, un peu bête, mais difficile à découvrir et lourde à porter. ... Les hommes meurent et ils ne sont pas heureux.*'

C. p. 110. '*de la lune, ou de l'immortalité, de quelque chose qui soit dément peut-être, mais qui ne soit pas de ce monde.*'

C. p. 124. '*lorsque tout sera aplani, l'impossible enfin sur terre, la lune dans mes mains, alors, peut-être, moi-même je serai transformé et le monde avec moi, alors enfin les hommes ne mourront pas et ils seront heureux.*'

p. 16. Cf. Anthony Curtis, *New Developments in the French Theatre*, London, The Curtain Press, 1948, p. 31.

C. p. 211. '*Je n'ai pas pris la voie qu'il fallait ... ma liberté n'est pas la bonne.*'

C. p. 196. '*dort deux heures toutes les nuits et le reste du temps, incapable de reposer, erre dans les galeries de son palais.*' This detail, like several others, is taken directly from Suetonius.

p. 17. C. p. 201. '*Chasse au bonheur qui fait les êtres purs*
            Ciel où le soleil ruisselle,
      Fêtes uniques et sauvages, mon délire sans espoir'

p. 18. '*La non-garantie des valeurs*'—'the impossibility of justifying moral values' is one possible translation for this phrase of Claude-Edmonde Magny in *La Littérature française depuis 1940*, *France-libre*, 15.2.45, p. 107. The rest of the quotation is interesting because it shows how French critics of the immediate post-war period sympathized with Camus's problems, and took them very seriously. This '*non-garantie des valeurs*' was, she wrote, 'a philosophical shock compared to which the discovery in the eighteenth century of the plurality of worlds, in the nineteenth of the evolution of species, were as nothing. The Kantian critique has taken more than a century to attain the final development of its philosophical consequences. One must admit that it has succeeded with remarkable thoroughness.'

CHAPTER TWO

p. 19. Cf. *L'Énigme. L'Été*, 1954. p. 132.

Combat 3.11.44. Reprinted in *Actuelles* 1 (1950). '*Non, tout ne se résume pas dans la négation et l'absurdité. Mais il faut d'abord passer par la négation et l'absurdité parce que ce sont elles que notre génération a rencontrées et dont nous avons à nous arranger.*' '*Il s'agit de savoir pour nous, si l'homme, sans le secours de l'éternel ou de la pensée rationaliste, peut créer à lui seul ses propres valeurs,*' same article.

p. 20. Cf. *France-Observateur*, 5.6.52. '*des centaines de pages, que je tiens à votre disposition et qui prouvent que, même lorsque M. Hervé et ses amis l'abandonnaient pour des raisons de tactique, je n'ai* *jamais mené réellement d'autre lutte politique que celle-là.*' More details of this dispute are given later in the notes.

Combat. 24.11.44. '*La justice sociale peut très bien se faire sans une philosophie ingénieuse.*'

Combat. 21.8.44. '*par le simple réflexe d'un honneur humilié.*'

p. 21. L. p. 75-76. '*à la vérité, moi qui croyais penser comme vous, je ne voyais guère d'argument à vous opposer sinon un goût violent de la justice qui, pour finir, me paraissait aussi peu raisonné que la plus soudaine des passions.*' The ideas expressed in these letters follow almost exactly the argument between Cherea and Caligula in *Caligula*, Act III, scene 6. This fact has led several critics to say that Camus altered the 1938 text of *Caligula* before putting it on the stage in 1945.

L. p. 78. '*J'ai choisi la justice pour rester fidèle à la terre. Je continue à croire que le monde n'a pas de sens supérieur. Mais je sais que quelque chose en lui a du sens, et c'est l'homme parce qu'il est le seul être à exiger d'en avoir.*'

N. p. 80-81 '*Seul contre la colonne, j'étais comme quelqu'un qu'on prend à la gorge et qui crie sa foi comme une dernière parole. Tout en moi protestait contre une semblable résignation. "Il faut", disaient les inscriptions. Mais non, et ma révolte avait raison. Cette joie qui allait, indifférente et absorbée comme un pèlerin sur la terre, il me fallait la suivre pas à pas.*'

p. 22. MS. p. 77. '*confrontement perpétuel de l'homme et de sa propre obscurité ... exigence d'une impossible transcendance ... présence constante de l'homme et de lui-même. Elle n'est pas aspiration, elle est sans espoir.*'

Combat 24.8.44 and 8.9.44. '*la dimension de l'espoir et la profondeur de la révolte*' '*La justice, au contraire, et Paris vient de l'éprouver dans ses nuits illuminées de l'insurrection, ne va pas sans la révolte.*'

p. 23. *Combat* 19.9.44. '*le refus entier, obstiné, presque aveugle au début, d'un ordre qui voulait mettre les hommes à genoux. ... La révolte, c'est d'abord le coeur.*'

p. 24. RR. p. 9. '*On voit déjà que l'affirmation de la révolte s'étend à quelque chose qui transcende l'individu, qui le tire de sa solitude supposée, et qui fonde une valeur.*'
cf. MS. p. 17.

RR. p. 11. '*C'est dans la révolte que l'homme se dépasse dans autrui, et, de ce point de vue, la solidarité humaine est métaphysique.*'

RR. p. 22. '*la seule question qui nous paraisse de quelque import-ance; l'homme peut-il seul, et sans le recours de l'éternel, créer ses propres valeurs?' 'il y a un au-delà de l'angoisse hors de l'éternité, et c'est la révolte.' 'la plus relative des expériences, érigée en absolu.'*

RR. pp. 18-19. *'une conversion au relatif qui signifierait fidélité à la condition humaine.'*

p. 25. RR. p. 17. *'cela n'est jamais possible, mais le désespoir recommence avec la négation de la première vérité apportée par la révolte, à savoir que l'homme n'est pas seul.' 'entêtement dans la condition limitée de la créature.'*

p. 26. *Combat* 23.11.44. *'libéral, mal formulé quoique généreux.' 'l'amélioration obstinée, chaotique mais inévitable de la condition humaine.'*

RR. p. 14, and HR. p. 34. *'un ordre humain où toutes les réponses soient humaines, c'est-à-dire, raisonnablement formulées'*

CHAPTER THREE

p. 29. RR. p. 18. *'Dans un monde absurde, la révolté garde encore une certitude. C'est la solidarité des hommes dans une même aventure, le fait que l'épicier et lui sont tous les deux frustrés.'*

RR. p. 18. *'le mal qui éprouvait un seul homme est devenu peste collective.'*

p. 30. Grand the real hero of the novel, cf. P. p. 156. *'Oui, s'il est vrai que les hommes tiennent à se proposer des exemples et des modèles, et s'il faut absolument qu'il y en ait un dans cette histoire, le narrateur propose justement ce héros insignifiant et effacé qui n'avait pour lui qu'un peu de bonté au coeur, et un idéal apparemment ridicule.'*

p. 31. P. p. 337. *'pour le malheur et l'enseignement des hommes, la peste réveillerait ses rats et les enverrait mourir dans les rues d'une cité heureuse.'*

P. p. 241. *'Le salut de l'homme est un trop grand mot pour moi. Je ne vais pas si loin. C'est sa santé qui m'intéresse, sa santé d'abord.'*

p. 32. RR. p. 19. *'révolte métaphysique au même titre que l'élan spectaculaire qui dresse Byron devant Dieu.'*

P. p. 147. *'lutter contre la mort sans lever les yeux vers le ciel où il se tait.'* This passage has frequently been quoted to show a similarity of thought between Camus and Alfred de Vigny. It recalls the closing lines of *Le Mont des Oliviers:*—

> *'Le juste opposera le dédain à l'absence*
> *Et ne répondra plus que par un froid silence*
> *Au silence éternel de la divinité.'*

There are other points of resemblance between Camus and Vigny. Both have a basic metaphysical pessimism, from which they escape in the ideal of service to man (Cf. Vigny, *La Bouteille à la Mer*), both regard man as being a stranger in an indifferent and possibly hostile universe (Cf. Vigny, *La Maison du Berger*), both are horrified by intolerance and systematic violence, and both consider intolerance to come from an excessive belief in abstract ideas and from political ruthlessness (Cf. *Stello* and *Cinq Mars*). The idea of revolt in Vigny's work differs considerably, however, from that in Camus's (Cf. Georges Bonnefoy, *Les Idées morales et religieuses d'Alfred de Vigny*, 1945).

p. 33. P. p. 81. '*la souffrance principale de ce long temps d'exil.*'

P. p. 82. '*enfoncés dans la stupide confiance humaine*'. In 1947 Camus wrote a preface to the posthumous edition of the poems by his friend René Leynaud, with whom he had worked in the Resistance movement and who had been killed by the Germans. On their last meeting, Camus said, they both made plans for their future, and were both so far from thinking of an eternal separation that he could not even remember Leynaud's last words. '*Enfoncé dans la stupide confiance humaine, sur de lui et de ses lendemains, je l'ai seulement salué d'un bout du pont à l'autre.*'

C. p. 195. '*C'est moi qui remplace la peste*'; also Cherea on p. 189.

P. p. 325. '*ce peuple abasourdi dont tous les jours une partie, entassée dans la gueule d'un four, s'évaporait en fumée grasse, pendant que l'autre, chargée des chaînes de l'impuissance et de la peur, attendait son tour*' (It is this passage which seems inspired by Pascal—see note on p. 12.)

p. 34. The section beginning '*Un des résultats les plus remarquables de la fermeture des portes ...*' was published in *Domaine français* in Geneva in 1943, under the title of *Les Exilés dans la Peste*.

P. p. 111. '*Mes frères, vous êtes dans le malheur, mes frères, vous l'avez mérité.*' These are the opening words of Paneloux's first sermon.

Combat 22.12.44. '*Cette époque est celle de la séparation.*'

p. 35. L. p. 27-28. '*Il nous a fallu tout ce temps pour aller voir si nous avions le droit de tuer les hommes, s'il nous était permis d'ajouter à l'atroce misère de ce monde.*' Camus here introduces a certain distortion into history by projecting his own ideas onto it. He attributes the length of the fight against Nazism to the fact that the French needed a long time to overcome their scruples—which is, as he says of Lautréamont's ideas on Christ, '*historiquement hasardé*' (HR. p. 113).

p. 36. P. p. 275. '*Je ne voulais pas être un pestiféré.*' '*je n'avais pas cessé d'être un pestiféré pendant toutes ces longues années, ou, pourtant, de toute mon âme, je croyais lutter justement contre la peste.*' '*cette dégoûtante boucherie.*' '*du côté des victimes ... pour limiter les dégâts.*'

P. p. 315. '*rester sur le rivage, les mains vides et le coeur tordu, sans armes et sans secours encore une fois contre le désastre.*'

p. 37. *Ni Victimes ni Bourreaux* first appeared in *Combat* between 19th and 30th November 1946. They were reproduced in the socialist review *Caliban* in November 1947, and in the first volume of *Actuelles* in 1950. In French, the quotation is '*un monde ou le meurtre est légitimé et ou la vie humaine est considéré comme futile*'.

Article published in *Terre des Hommes* on 26.1.46, entitled *La Réforme de l'Enseignement*: '*Quand on croit, comme Hegel et toute la philosophie moderne, que l'homme est fait pour l'histoire et non pas l'histoire pour l'homme, on ne peut pas croire au dialogue. On croit à l'efficacité et à la volonté de puissance, c'est-à-dire, au silence et au mensonge. À la limite, on croit au meurtre.*'

P. p. 150. '*la bonne volonté peut faire autant de dégâts que la méchanceté si elle n'est pas éclairée.*'

p. 38. P. p. 278. '*tout le malheur des hommes vient de ce qu'ils ne tenaient pas un langage clair.*'

In an interview published in *Paru*, No. 47, 1948, pp. 7-13, Camus said, '*Les écrivains sont du côté de la vie, contre la mort et le mal. C'est la seule justification de leur étrange métier.*' It was in this interview that he said he preferred Rieux's attitude as '*une possibilité humaine, strictement humaine*'.

P. p. 157. '*juste après, et jamais avant, l'exigence généreuse du bonheur.*'

P. p. 330. '*un coeur ignorant, c'est-à-dire, solitaire.*'

CHAPTER FOUR

p. 41. ES. *Avertissement,* '*toutes les formes d'expression dramatique, depuis le monologue lyrique jusqu'au théâtre collectif, en passant par le jeu muet, le simple dialogue, la farce et le choeur.*'

p. 42. ES. p. 92. '*... la ridicule angoisse du bonheur, le visage stupide des amoureux, la contemplation égoiste des paysages et la coupable ironie.*'

ES. p. 93. '*Vous avez vos fiches, vous ne mourrez plus par caprice.*

Le destin, désormais, s'est assagi, et il a pris ses bureaux. Vous serez dans la statistique, et vous allez enfin servir à quelque chose.'
'le silence, l'ordre, et l'absolue justice'.

ES. p. 189. *'La suppression, voilà mon évangile, mais jusqu'ici je n'avais pas de bonnes raisons. Maintenant, j'ai la raison réglementaire.'*

p. 43. ES. p. 178. *'Du plus loin que je m'en souviens, il a toujours suffi qu'un homme surmonte sa peur pour que la machine commence à grincer.'*

ES. p. 211. *'On ne peut pas être heureux sans consentir à la mort des autres. C'est la justice de cette terre.' 'Je ne suis pas né pour consentir à cette justice-là. ... Je connais la recette. Il faut tuer pour supprimer le meurtre, violenter pour guérir l'injustice. Il y a des siècles que cela dure! Il y a des siècles que les seigneurs de ta race pourrissent la plaie du monde sous prétexte de la guérir, et continuent de vanter leur recette, puisque personne ne leur rit au nez.'*

ES. p. 220. *'Je me suis gâté la main que j'avais quelquefois secourable.'*

p. 44. ES. p. 233 *'Je sais trop de choses. Même le mépris a fait son temps. Adieu, braves gens, vous apprendrez cela un jour qu'on ne peut bien vivre en sachant que l'homme n'est rien et que la face de Dieu est affreuse.'*

ES. p. 144. *'Le droit de ceux qui aiment à ne pas être séparés, le droit des coupables à être pardonnés et des repentis à être honorés.'*

p. 45. The reply to Gabriel Marcel's *Pourquoi l'Espagne?* was published in *Combat* in 1948 and reprinted in *Actuelles* in 1950. Camus insisted that he refused to excuse *'cette peste hideuse à l'Ouest parce qu'elle exerce ses ravages à l'Est'*. He has constantly attacked Franco's dictatorship in Spain, and in 1956 wrote a preface to a collection of poems and articles written by Spanish political exiles. His mother was Spanish.

The article *Les Meurtriers délicats* was published in *La Table Ronde*, No. 1, 1948, pp. 42-50, and translated in *World Review* in November 1949.

J. p. 41. *'Nous tuons pour bâtir un monde où plus personne ne sera tuée.'*

p. 46. J. p. 77. *'... ceux qui vivent aujourd'hui sur la même terre que moi' 'pour une lointaine patrie dont je ne suis même pas sûr' 'je n'irai pas ajouter à l'injustice vivante pour une justice morte.'*

J. p. 74 and p. 79. *'une terre de liberté qui finira par recouvrir le monde entier.' 'c'est tuer pour rien, parfois, que de ne pas tuer assez.'*

J. p. 168. *'D'autres viendront qui s'autoriseront de nous pour tuer et ne paieront pas de leur vie.'*

'*Entre le oui et le non*' is the title of one of the essays in *L'Envers et l'Endroit*. (This particular essay was translated in *Partisan Review*, November 1949.) In Camus's early work, he says 'Yes' to the passion for physical existence, and 'No' to any creed or set of beliefs which will make him consent to the inevitability of death or accept any unjustifiable solution to the problem of the absurd. In his work after 1945, the 'No' is addressed to all systems of oppression, and the 'Yes' to the instincts which prompt him to take part in any political activity which seems likely to improve the human lot. Camus is much attracted by images of tension and balance, and the closing image of *L'Homme révolté* is based upon them.

The discussion between Kaliayev and Stepan is at times reminiscent of the difference which separates Brutus from Cassius. What, however, for Shakespeare, was a question of temperament and character, is for Camus one of political and philosophical principles.

p. 47. J. p. 161. '*La mort sera ma suprême protestation contre un monde fait de larmes et de sang.*'

J. p. 169. '*C'est facile, tellement plus facile de mourir de ses contradictions que de les vivre.*'

J. p. 137. '*J'aime la beauté, le bonheur, c'est pour cela que je hais le despotisme.*'

J. p. 149. '*Nous ne sommes pas au monde, nous sommes des justes. Il y a une chaleur qui n'est pas pour nous. Ah, pitié pour les justes!*'

J. p. 149. '*Ceux qui s'aiment aujourd'hui doivent mourir ensemble s'ils veulent être réunis! L'injustice sépare, la honte sépare, la douleur, le mal qu'on fait aux autres, le vivre sépare. Vivre est une torture puisque vivre sépare.*'

p. 48. *L'Exhortation aux Médecins de la Peste*, p. 150. '*D'une façon générale, observez la mesure qui est la première ennemie de la peste et la règle naturelle de l'homme. Némésis n'était point, comme on vous l'a dit dans les écoles, la déesse de la vengeance, mais celle de la mesure.*'

L'Exil d'Hélène. Reprinted in *Été* (1954), p. 109. '*À l'aurore de la pensée grecque, Héraclite imaginait déjà que la justice pose ses bornes à l'univers physique lui-même.*' p. 108. '*L'Europe, lancée à la conquête de la totalité, est fille de la démesure.*' This essay has been translated and published in the same volume as Justin O'Brien's translation of *Le Mythe de Sisyphe* (Hamish Hamilton, 1955).

HR. p. 22. '*l'histoire de l'orgueil européen.*' An interesting comparison can be made between Camus and a Christian thinker like le Père De Lubac, whose book *Le Drame de l'Humanisme athée* (Spès 1944. Translated by Edith M. Riley, Sheed and Ward, 1949) lays the same insistence upon the theme of the 'divinisation of man'. Although Camus shares De Lubac's idea that this divinisation is accomplished only at the price of the sacrifice of the individual, he does not, of course, go so far as to repeat the thesis of De Lubac that a city constructed against man. Camus is trying, in *L'Homme révolté*, to correct the excesses of atheistic revolution without having recourse to Christian morals. Nevertheless, he does come very near the Christian thinkers in his insistence upon the need for a fidelity in revolt and for certain values. Camus has always been discussed with great tolerance and understanding by Christian thinkers, with whom he is in agreement on many points. I have, myself, heard a sermon preached in the chapel of King's College, London, which quoted extensively from *La Peste*. Camus's objections to Christianity are first of all that he cannot accept the idea that a good and merciful God should allow the innocent to suffer, and secondly that in the days of its power and influence, the Christian Church persecuted heretics with almost the same vigour as the Communist party of to-day. His reasons for not being a Christian are not at all intellectual, and are far removed from the rationalist attitude of a nineteenth-century thinker like Renan. In an article published in *Les Cahiers du Sud*, in April 1943 (pp. 306-311), Camus discussed the life of a priest, Father Pouget, who had spent his life in an attempt to find a compromise between blind faith and reasoning disbelief on the problem of the contradictions in the Bible. Camus wrote that 'the problem of faith does not lie in quibbles ('*arguties*') of this kind'. For him, the quarrel between science and religion has no reality, and he writes: 'In fact, modern unbelief is no longer based on science as it was at the end of the last century. It denies the faith of science as much as that of religion. It is no longer the scepticism of reason in the face of miracles, but rather a passionate unbelief ('*une incroyance passionnée*').'

CHAPTER FIVE

p. 50. Camus himself admitted to me that he was not satisfied with it as a work of art, and agreed that outside France it was likely to be difficult to understand. He rather modestly added that he could not explain how it managed to sell almost 70,000 copies. It probably holds the record, for a book of its length, in the number of proper names which it contains. There are 276 in all, made up of 160 names of authors and artists—ranging from Rimbaud to Milton and Petrus Borel to Bossuet—96 historical characters—including Christ, Stalin,

Ford, Napoleon and St Paul—and 20 fictional and mythical. The number of pages on which various characters are named is interesting to note. Marx, 57. Hegel, 48. Nietzsche, 36. Sade, 27. Ivan Karamazov, 18. Stalin, 6.

The opening passage of *L'Homme révolté* appeared in the first number of *Empédocle*, 1949, pp. 19-27. '*Le meurtre et l'absurde.*'

Nietzsche et le Nihilisme appeared in *Les Temps Modernes*, August 1951, pp. 88-97.

Lautréamont et la Banalité in *Les Cahiers du Sud*, No. 307, 1951, pp. 399-405.

La Remarque sur la Révolte is textually almost the same as pp. 25-36 of *L'Homme révolté*.

It should be noted that the English translation of *L'Homme révolté* omits several passages of the French text.

In an interview in *La Gazette des Lettres* in February 1952, Camus said that *L'Homme révolté* was '*une confession ... la seule sorte au moins dont je suis capable*'. At the beginning of the interview, Pierre Berger said that he had lost faith in man, but found it again on reading *L'Homme révolté*.

p. 52. '*les royaumes de nécessité absolue*'; this phrase does not occur in the text of *L'Homme révolté*, but in a letter to *Arts* on 23.11.51.

p. 53. HR. p. 122. '*ils préféraient encore le pire. En cela, ils étaient nihilistes. ... La vraie déstruction du langage que le surréalisme a souhaitée avec tant d'obstination ne réside pas dans l'incohérence ou l'automatisme. Elle réside dans le mot d'ordre.*'

RR. p. 18. '*La seule révolution a la mesure de l'homme doit résider dans une conversion au relatif qui signifierait exactement la fidélité à la condition humaine.*'

p. 54. HR. p. 301. '*Le vrai, l'éternel Prométhée a pris maintenant le visage d'une de ses victimes. Le même cri, venu du fond des âges, retentit toujours au fond du désert de Scythie.*'

p. 55. HR. p. 45. '*L'idée de l'innocence opposée à la culpabilité, la vision d'une histoire tout entière résumée à la lutte du bien et du mal leur était étrangère. Dans leur univers, il y avait plus de fautes que de crimes, le seul crime définitif étant la démesure.*'

HR. p. 45. '*Dans le monde totalement historique qui menace d'être le nôtre, il n'y a plus de fautes, au contraire, il n'y a que des crimes, dont le premier est la mesure.*'

HR. p. 53. '*un innocent de plus, que les représentants du Dieu d'Abraham ont sacrifié spectaculairement.*' '*Ainsi se trouve déblayé le terrain pour la grande offensive contre le ciel ennemi.*'

p. 56. RR. p. 23. '*une oeuvre idéale où la création soit corrigée.*'

HR. p. 320. '*La Comédie humaine, c'est l'Imitation de Dieu le*

Père.' In his *Histoire de la Littérature française*, NRF 1936, Thibaudet speaks of '*cette* Imitation *de Dieu le Père latente dans la* Comédie Humaine' (p. 221). The actual form which Camus gives to the quotation, (with *Imitation* in italics) is a little difficult to understand.

'*L'art, quelque soit son but, fait toujours une coupable concurrence à Dieu.*'

p. 57. HR. p. 330. '*Le plus sur défi qu'une oeuvre de cette sorte puisse porter à la création est de se présenter comme un tout, un monde clos et unifié.*'

HR. p. 378. '*Tous peuvent revivre, en effet, auprès des sacrifiés de 1905, mais à la condition de comprendre qu'il se corrigent les uns les autres et qu'une limite, sous le soleil, les arrête tous. Chacun dit à l'autre qu'il n'est pas Dieu; ici s'achève le romantisme.*'

p. 59. Daniel-Rops, writing in a special number of *La Nef*, June-July 1951, on *Le Mal du Siècle*, p. 200.

Jean-Jacques Rivière, *La Nef*, August 1947, p. 142. This phrase occurs in a not very favourable review of *La Peste*.

Albert Ollivier, in *L'Arche*, Oct.-Nov. 1944. Review of *Le Mythe de Sisyphe* and *L'Étranger*.

p. 60. Claude Mauriac made this criticism in his review of *L'Homme révolté* in *La Table Ronde*, December 1951. In fact, Camus does mention Malraux in a footnote on page 71, but does not deal with him in any detail. Camus shows a certain reluctance in both *Le Mythe de Sisyphe* and *L'Homme révolté* to discuss other French writers.

p. 61. '*J'ai vécu le nihilisme, la contradiction, la violence et le vertige de la destruction.*' This was in a letter to *Le Libertaire*, reprinted in *Actuelles* II, 1953, p. 83.

Camus said in the interview with Berger that he had spent four years in composing it.

In *Combat*, 11.9.44, Camus wrote: '*Le pays n'a pas besoin de Talleyrand ou de Bergery. Il a besoin de Saint-Just.*' The article, *Le Socialisme mystifié*, in *Ni Victimes ni Bourreaux* shows that this desire was not long-lived. The actual choice to deal at such length with the Marquis de Sade and with Saint-Just was probably determined by the fact that both of these writers had received a great deal of critical attention since the war, and were well in the public's mind. Several communist selections from Saint-Just's work had been published with prefaces designed to show how the example of Saint-Just should inspire modern revolutionaries to an equal ruthlessness and ardour. Sade had first of all been adopted by the surrealists as the ideal rebel, but had achieved even greater notoriety since 1945 as a result of the studies on him by Maurice Blanchot, Pierre Klossowski, Maurice

Nadeau, Georges Bataille, Gilbert Lély, and Jean Paulhan. As in *Le Mythe de Sisyphe*, Camus chooses in *L'Homme révolté* to talk about writers who are fashionable.

p. 62. Camus's conception of revolt is really based upon an isolated incident of the individual slave refusing to obey an order. He quotes to support his argument the case of the prisoners in the Chinese revolution and the Russian salt-mines who committed suicide as a protest against the ill-treatment of their companions. It does not, in spite of the great nobility of the action which Camus describes, necessarily follow that it is a universal reaction upon which a universal code of values can be based. One might argue with the same amount of *logic*, that the attitude of those whom cowardice kept silent and alive, and who accepted humiliation, was an equally universal one. Camus's philosophical arguments are often too formal and abstract to be persuasive in a general context, and a critical analysis of the opening passage of *La Remarque sur la Révolte* could show that it was merely a verbal jingle.

The famous quarrel between Sartre and Camus was not, as Richard Wollheim suggested in *The Cambridge Journal* in October 1953 (pp. 3-19) an example of the 'Political Philosophy of Existentialism'. As early as 1945 Camus had declared that he was not an existentialist, and protested violently against a critic who said that *Caligula* was an illustration of Sartre's philosophy. The real quarrel was on the question of ends and means, which goes further back than the vogue of existentialism.

In No. 3 of *Les Temps Modernes*, 1945, pp. 574-576, Albert Ollivier praised Camus for having succeeded in expressing the static nature of the absurd in a play.

In November 1947, Etiemble, pp. 911-920, criticized *La Peste*, and Pouillon, pp. 921-929. p. 925 '*le roman de la résistance telle qu'on aurait voulu qu'elle fût*'—and not, as it was in reality, a kind of civil war.

p. 63. Jeanson's review was published in the May number of *Les Temps Modernes* in 1952, pp. 2070-2090. '*Albert Camus ou l'âme révoltée.*'

Camus's reply, *Lettre au Directeur des Temps Modernes*, in August 1952, pp. 334-353, was followed by two replies, one by Sartre and one by Jeanson.

p. 64. p. 327. '*Oui ou non*, La Phénoménologie de l'esprit *autorise-t-elle une théorie de cynisme politique, et, par exemple, y a-t-il eu des Hégéliens de gauche et ces derniers ont-ils influencé en ce sens le développement du communisme au vingtième siècle?*' When M. Camus read through the original text of this study, he noted in the margin, '*Oui, cela est, et cela continue d'être la question.*' (August 1956)

p. 65. Claude Mauriac in *La Table Ronde*, December 1951, pp. 98-109. Mauriac, like Sartre, raises the question of Camus's originality in *L'Homme révolté*. He points out that the substance of Camus's arguments against Marxism is to be found in writers like Jules Monnerot and Roger Caillois. This is certainly true, and Camus acknowledges his debt to these thinkers in footnotes in *L'Homme révolté*. Possibly more important than that of these right-wing thinkers is the influence of Jean Grenier, who was Camus's teacher at Algiers, and to whom *L'Homme révolté* is dedicated. Camus recommends Grenier's book *L'Age des orthodoxies* (Gallimard, 1936) in a footnote, and the central theme of his criticism of communism is already expressed in Grenier's book *Le Choix* (1941). Grenier condemns the Hegelian dialectic as '*Hybris qu'ont connue et condamnée les Grecs. ... Cette monstrueuse dialectique ... qui sépare les hommes qu'elle prétend unir*' (*Le Choix*, p. 34). The originality of Camus's thought in *L'Homme révolté* lies not so much in the actual ideas expressed as in the fact that they are expressed from the point of view of revolt, and by a man who has shown by his earlier work that he understands the spiritual dilemma of his time.

p. 66. Cf. Michel Carrouges, *André Breton et les données fondamentales du surréalisme* (Gallimard, 1950), '*une révolte radicale contre cette civilisation* (i.e. of France) *asservie par les philosophies abstraites, les arts classiques, la mentalité bourgeoise, et les économies travaillistes*' (Introduction). Cf. also pp. 11-12, the surrealist poets '*prêchent la révolte contre la condition humaine et proclament l'espérance d'une nouvelle transfiguration de la vie par la magie poétique*'.
André Breton in *Arts*, 12.10.51.

p. 67. Camus in *Arts*, 23.11.51: '*Nous avons tous compris alors qu'un certain nihilisme dont nous étions tous plus ou moins solidaires, nous laissait sans défense contre une entreprise que nous détestions de tout notre être;*' and *Arts*, 19.10.51: '*Si je voyais quelque chose à conserver dans notre société, je ne verrais aucun déshonneur à être conservateur. Malheureusement, il n'en est rien.*' '*un certain conformisme révolté aussi contraire à la vraie révolte que la nuit l'est au jour.*'

p. 68. *Arts*, 16.11.51. '*Il s'agissait—métaphysiquement parlant—d'un attentat savant contre l'homme qui fût de nature à atteindre à la fois le "je" et "l'autre".*' The implied quotation is from Rimbaud's *Lettre du Voyant*, '*Car Je est un autre*'. This remark of Breton's fits in with the declared aim of surrealism to obliterate the existence of opposites.
Bataille, *Critique*, December 1951, p. 1019, and January, pp. 29-41.

For Bataille's ideas on *La Peste*, and on true revolt, cf. *La Morale du Malheur*, *Critique*, June-July 1947, pp. 3-15.

L'Esprit, November 1947, pp. 615-621. *De la Peste ou d'un nouvel humanitarisme.*

p. 69. *L'Esprit*, 1952, pp. 736-746, p. 743.

The communist journalist Pierre Hervé, who has since left the party, wrote a criticism of *L'Homme révolté* in *La Nouvelle Critique* in April 1952, pp. 66-76, entitled *La Révolte camuse*. A single quotation (p. 76) gives the general tone of the review. Hervé speaks of *'les escrocs qui se prétendent héritiers du syndicalisme révolutionnaire afin de recevoir des subventions en dollars'*. This article by Hervé was described by Lebar, writing in the left-wing review *L'Observateur*, as *'remarquable'*, an adjective which he intended to be quietly ironic. This description annoyed Camus, who wrote a violent letter to *L'Observateur* demanding that the adjective—which he had misread as *'belle'*—should be withdrawn (*L'Observateur*, 5.6.52). Roger Stéphane replied that Camus had made a mistake and that in any case his demand that *L'Observateur* should in all cases ally itself with what he, Camus, thought was right, constituted too strong a demand. Camus's extreme susceptibility in this matter laid him open to Sartre's taunt of *'Dites-moi, mon cher Camus, par quel miracle ne peut-on discuter vos livres sans ôter ses raisons de vivre à l'humanité?'* It was rather inconsiderate of Camus to criticise *L'Observateur*, since its editor, Claude Bourget, had on the 13th and 20th of December 1951, written a most enthusiastic review of *L'Homme révolté*, welcoming it as *'ce livre précieux où presque rien n'est à reprendre d'une implacable analyse'* and saw that there might be deduced from it the most useful notion of *'un Marxisme véritablement scientifique et "probabiliste", aussi efficace que l'ancien à détruire les hypocrisies sociales, mieux adapté à se servir, pour prévoir et planifier, non de dogmes momentanés et meurtriers, mais d'hypothèses de travail, comme font les vrais savants'*. This article is in the strongest possible contrast to the review which appeared in *The New Statesman and Nation* on January 16th, 1954, by R. H. S. Crossman. Entitling his article *A Frustrated Intellectual*, Crossman put Camus firmly in his place as a distinguished literary man whose opinions on politics were about as much use as Crossman's own opinions on Proust. *L'Observateur* and the *New Statesman* have almost exactly the same political line.

p. 70. Marcel Thiébaut in *La Revue de Paris*, August 1947.

Roger Stéphane in *La Revue Internationale*, No. 16, 1947.

La Nef, August 1947, pp. 141-143, and p. 149.

Cf. Michel Laparade, *Réflexions sur quatre médecins de roman:*

essai de définition d'un humanisme médical contemporain, Bordeaux, 1948.

p. 72. *The Liberal Imagination*, Secker and Warburg, 1951, p. 301.

CHAPTER SIX

p. 74. *La Ballade de la Géôle de Reading*, translated by Jacques Bour, published by Falaize in 1953. Preface, *L'Artiste en Prison*, pp. 11-25). Preface translated in *Encounter*.

p. 76. *La Chute*, p. 11. '*Une seule phrase leur* (future historians) *suffira pour l'homme moderne; il forniquait et lisait des journaux.*'

p. 77. Donat O'Donnell in a talk on the B.B.C. Third Programme, in January 1957.

L'Énigme, p. 132. '*Dans la mesure où cela est possible, j'aurais aimé être, au contraire, un écrivain objectif. J'appelle objectif un auteur qui se propose des sujets sans jamais se prendre lui-même comme objet.*' Clearly Camus has not always been completely objective, and these remarks seem to contradict what he said elsewhere about *L'Homme révolté* and *La Peste* being personal confessions. It may be that, once again like Gide, Camus's declarations as to the meaning of his different books may vary as he passes through different stages.

p. 78. *La Gazette littéraire* (Geneva), 27th March, 1954, interview with Francis Jotterand. '*On a trop affirmé l'innocence de la création. Aujourd'hui, on veut nous accabler sous le poids de notre culpabilité. Il y a, je crois, une vérité intermédiaire.*'

La Chute, p. 162. '*Couvert de cendres, m'arrachant lentement les cheveux, le visage labouré par les ongles, mais le regard perçant, je me tiens devant l'humanité entière, récapitulant mes hontes, sans perdre de vue l'effet que je produis, et disant: "J'étais le dernier des derniers." Alors, insensiblement, je passe, dans mon discours, du "je" au "nous". Quand j'arrive au "voilà ce que nous sommes", le tour est joué, je peux leur dire leurs vérités. Je suis comme eux, bien entendu, nous sommes dans le même bouillon. J'ai cependant une supériorité, celle de le savoir, qui me donne le droit de parler. Vous voyez l'avantage, j'en suis sûr. Plus je m'accuse et plus j'ai le droit de vous juger. Mieux, je vous provoque à vous juger vous-même, ce qui me soulage d'autant.*'

p. 79. *La Chute*, p. 153. '*Vous voyez en moi, très cher, un partisan éclairé de la servitude.*'

La Chute, p. 169. '*ma carrière de faux prophète qui crie dans le désert et refuse d'en sortir.*'

'brings many middle-class intellectuals to communism', etc.—This is the explanation which M. Camus gave me himself in conversation in August 1956.

p. 81. *La Femme adultère* was first published in 1954 in Algiers.

L'Exil et le Royaume, p. 32. '*seigneurs misérables et libres d'un étrange royaume.*' '*Janine ne savait pas pourquoi cette idée l'emplissait d'une tristesse si douce et si vaste qu'elle lui fermait les yeux. Elle savait seulement que ce royaume, de tout temps, lui avait été promis et que jamais, pourtant, il ne serait le sien, sinon à ce fugitif instant, peut-être, où elle rouvrit les yeux sur le ciel soudain immobile et sur les flots de lumière figée, pendant que les voix qui montaient de la ville arabe se taisaient brusquement. Il lui sembla que le cours du monde venait alors de s'arrêter et que personne, à partir de cet instant, ne vieillirait plus ni ne mourrait. En tous lieux, désormais, la vie était suspendue, sauf dans son coeur où, au même moment, quelqu'un pleurait de peine et d'émerveillement.*'

p. 82. Cf. *La Chute*, p. 166. '*Oh, soleil, plages, et les îles sous les alizés, jeunesse dont le souvenir me désespère.*'

L'Exil et le Royaume, p. 39. '*Aucun souffle, aucun bruit, sinon, parfois, le crépitement étouffé des pierres que le froid réduisait en sable, ne venait troubler la solitude et le silence qui entouraient Janine. Au bout d'un instant, pourtant, il lui sembla qu'une sorte de giration pesante entraînait le ciel au-dessus d'elle. Dans les épaisseurs de la nuit sèche et froide, des milliers d'étoiles se formaient sans trêve et leurs glaçons étincelants, aussitôt détachés, commençaient de glisser insensiblement vers l'horizon. Janine ne pouvait s'arracher à la contemplation de ces feux à la dérive. Elle tournait avec eux et le même cheminement immobile la réunissait peu à peu à son être le plus profond, où le froid et le désir maintenant se combattaient. Devant elle, les étoiles tombaient, une à une, puis s'éteignaient parmi les pierres du désert, et à chaque fois Janine s'ouvrait un peu plus à la nuit. Elle respirait, elle oubliait le froid, le poids des êtres, la vie démente ou figée, la longue angoisse de vivre et de mourir. Après tant d'années où, fuyant devant la peur, elle avait couru follement, sans but, elle s'arrêtait enfin. En même temps, il lui semblait retrouver ses racines, la sève montait à nouveau dans son corps qui ne tremblait plus. Pressée de tout son ventre contre le parapet, tendue vers le ciel en mouvement, elle attendait seulement que son coeur encore bouleversé s'apaisât à son tour et que le silence se fît en elle. Les dernières étoiles des constellations laissèrent tomber leurs grappes un peu plus bas sur l'horizon du désert, et s'immobilisèrent. Alors, avec une douceur insupportable, l'eau de la nuit commença d'emplir Janine, submergea le froid, monta peu à peu du centre obscur de son être et déborda en flots ininterrompus jusqu'à sa bouche pleine de gémissements. L'instant après, le ciel entier s'étendait au-dessus d'elle, renversée sur la terre froide.'*

p. 84. Cf. the enquiry which *Combat* organized into the vogue of the American novel in France in January 1947, in which both Camus and Sartre explain their reasons for using an American technique in *L'Étranger* and *Le Sursis* respectively.

The first version of *Le Renégat* was published in the NNRF of June 1956.

p. 85. *L'Exil et le Royaume*, p. 48. '*Je n'avais compris que cela, une seule idée et mulet intelligent j'allais jusqu'au bout, j'allais au-devant des pénitences, je rognais sur l'ordinaire, enfin je voulais être un exemple, moi aussi pour qu'on me voie, et qu'en me voyant on rende hommage à ce qui m'avait rendu meilleur, à travers moi saluez mon Seigneur'* and p. 50. ... '*Puissant, oui, c'était le mot que, sans cesse, je roulais sur ma langue, je rêvais du pouvoir absolu, celui qui fait mettre genoux à terre, qui force l'adversaire à capituler, le convertit enfin, et plus l'adversaire est aveugle, sûr de lui, et plus son aveu proclame la royauté de celui qui a provoqué sa défaite.'*

p. 86. Cf. *Noces*, p. 47, footnote. '*Mon camarade Vincent, qui est tonnelier et champion de brasse junior, a une vue des choses encore plus claire. Il boit quand il a soif, s'il désire une femme cherche à coucher avec, et l'épouserait s'il l'aimait (ça n'est pas encore arrivé). Ensuite, il dit toujours; "Ça va mieux"—ce qui résume avec vigueur l'apologie qu'on pourrait faire de la satiété.'*

L'Exil et le Royaume, p. 76. '*L'eau profonde et claire, le fort soleil, les filles, la vie du corps, il n'y avait pas d'autre bonheur dans son pays. Et ce bonheur passait avec la jeunesse.'*

p. 88. *L'Exil et le Royaume*, p. 123. '*Tu as livré notre frère. Tu paieras'*, and p. 109, '*Une colère subite vint à Daru contre cet homme, contre tous les hommes et leur sale méchanceté, leurs haines inlassables, leur folie du sang.'*

p. 89. *L'Exil et le Royaume*, p. 146. '*Les disciples de Jonas lui expliquaient longuement ce qu'il avait peint, et pourquoi. Jonas découvrait ainsi dans son oeuvre beaucoup d'intentions qui le surprenaient un peu, et une foule de choses qu'il n'y avait pas mises.'*

p. 90. *Une Macumba au Brésil* appeared in the November number, 1951, of *Livres de France*, published by Hachette.

p. 91. Roger Quilliot's book was published by Gallimard in 1956. *L'Exil et le Royaume*, p. 202. '*Comme cela, oui, il y a un peuple. Mais ses maîtres sont des policiers ou des marchands.'*

p. 92. Cf. H.R Quotation from Hölderlin: '*Et ouvertement, je vouai mon coeur à la terre grave et souffrante, et souvent, dans la nuit sacrée, je lui promis de l'aimer fidèlement, jusqu'à la mort, sans peur, avec son lourd fardeau de fatalité, et de ne mépriser aucune de ses énigmes. Ainsi, je me liai à elle d'un lien mortel.*'

CHAPTER SEVEN

p. 94. In a special number of *Esprit, Les Carrefours de Camus,* January 1950, pp. 1-66. Rachel Bespaloff, *Le Monde du condamné à mort.*

A. J. Ayer. *Horizon*, March 1946, pp. 155-168. *Novelist-Philosophers No. 8. Albert Camus.* It is curious that no academic philosopher should have subjected Camus's work to a close analysis in France.

p. 96. Cf. Georges Blin, *Albert Camus ou le sens de l'absurde, Fontaine*, No. 30, 1943.

pp. 96-7. Cf. MS. p. 17, '*le caractère relatif de cet essai*'; p. 31, '*Ce qui m'intéresse, je veux encore le répéter, ce ne sont pas tant les découvertes absurdes*'; p. 40, '*il s'agit seulement de leurs découvertes*' '*il s'agit seulement de constater leur concordance*'; p. 45, '*c'est à cela qu'il faut se cramponner*' etc.

pp. 97-8. Cf. MS. pp. 75, 167, 121.

p. 98. Camus not an existentialist, Cf. *Les Nouvelles littéraires,* 15.11.45. '*Sartre et moi nous avons publié tous nos livres, sans exception, avant de nous connaître. Sartre est existentialiste, et le seul livre d'idées que j'ai publié était dirigé contre les philosophes dits existentialistes.*'

This remark is quoted by Pierre de Boisdeffre in his *Métamorphose de la littérature*, Ed. Alsatia, 1951, p. 275. '*Je ne me sens pas philosophe pour un sou; ce qui m'intéresse, c'est savoir comment il faut se conduire.*'

p. 99. MS. p. 27. '*Il arrive que les décors s'écroulent. Lever, tramway, quatre heures de bureau ou d'usine, repas, tramway, quatre heures de travail, repas, sommeil et lundi mardi mercredi jeudi vendredi et samedi sur le même rythme, cette route se suit aisément la plupart du temps. Un jour seulement, le "pourquoi" s'élève, et tout commence dans cette lassitude teintée d'étonnement.*' On page 165 Camus writes: '*L'ouvrier d'aujourd'hui travaille, tous les jours de sa vie, aux mêmes tâches et ce destin n'est pas moins absurde. Mais il n'est tragique* *qu'aux rares moments où il devient conscient. Sisyphe, prolétaire des dieux, impuissant et révolté, connaît toute l'étendue de sa misérable condition.'*

p. 104. Malraux, preface to *Le Temps du Mépris*, 1935.

MS. p. 167. *'Dans l'univers soudain réduit à son silence, les mille petites voix émerveillées de la terre s'élèvent.'*

HR. p. 377. *'Nous choisirons Ithaque, la terre fidèle, la pensée audacieuse et frugale, l'action lucide, la générosité de l'homme qui sait.'*

pp. 106-7. M. p. 79. *'Cela prouve que, dans un monde où tout peut se nier, il y a des forces indéniables et que sur cette terre où rien n'est assuré, nous avons nos certitudes. L'amour d'une mère pour son fils est maintenant ma certitude.' 'ce monde-ci n'est pas raisonnable, et je puis bien le dire, moi qui en ai tout goûté, depuis la création jusqu'à la destruction.'*

p. 108. Bernard Simiot, *Hommes et Mondes*, December 1948, pp. 712-716.

p. 109. L. p. 40. *'Nous voulions seulement aimer notre pays dans la justice, comme nous voulions l'aimer dans la vérité et dans l'espoir'*, and p. 78. *'Pour tout dire, vous avez choisi l'injustice, vous vous êtes mis avec les dieux. Votre logique n'était qu'apparente. J'ai choisi la justice, au contraire, pour rester fidèle à la terre. Je continue de croire que le monde n'a pas de sens supérieur. Mais je sais qu'il y a quelque chose en lui qui a du sens, et c'est l'homme, parce qu'il est le seul être à exiger d'en avoir.'*

p. 110. Cf. *Combat*, 19.11.46. *'Le XVII siècle a été le siècle des mathématiques, le XVIII celui des sciences physiques, et le XIX celui de la biologie. Notre siècle est le siècle de la peur.'*

p. 111. Wyndham Lewis, *The Writer and the Absolute*, Methuen 1952, p. 86.

p. 112. Etiemble, *La France Libre*, 15.11.45, p. 76.

Meursault as Christ—cf. letter to Pierre de Boisdeffre, quoted in *Métamorphose de la Littérature*, p. 269. *'De Meursault, homme-victime, bouc émissaire d'une société de Pharisiens et de Pilates, Camus ira jusqu'à nous dire qu'il est "le seul Christ que nous méritions".'*

p. 113. Cf. Et. pp. 86-88, p. 87. *'Je ne sentais plus que les cymbales du soleil sur mon front, et, indistinctement, le glaive étincelant jailli du couteau toujours en face de moi. ... La mer a charrié un souffle épais et ardent. ... La gâchette a cédé. ...'* At his trial, Meursault can only offer one reason for his act—Et. p. 146. *'J'ai dit rapidement, en mêlant un peu les mots et en me rendant compte de mon ridicule, que c'était à cause* *du soleil.*' This is the reason why he does not plead self-defence—he would be obliged to lie, and to say that it was because he thought the Arab was going to attack him with the knife that he fired, whereas in fact it was because of the sun. Yet it is one of the inconsistencies of the book that his lawyer should not have thought of pleading self-defence, especially in view of the fact that the Arab had already wounded Raymond.

p. 114. Cf. P. pp. 81-82.

p. 115. Cf. P. p. 200.

p. 116. Cf. P. p. 236.

p. 117. N. p. 13.

p. 118. Et. p. 94. '*Sans doute, j'aimais bien maman, mais cela ne voulait rien dire. Tous les êtres sains avaient plus ou moins désiré la mort de ceux qu'ils aimaient.*' Meursault's honesty disturbs the members of the legal profession with whom he comes into contact, for the '*juge d'instruction*', when told by Meursault that he does not believe in God, asks him, '*Voulez-vous que ma vie n'ait plus de sens?*'

p. 119. Cf. P. p. 315. '*rester sur le rivage, les mains vides et le coeur tordu, une fois de plus sans armes et sans secours contre le désastre.*'

p. 120. Cf. *World Review*, November 1949.

BIBLIOGRAPHY

(A) WORKS BY CAMUS PUBLISHED IN BOOK FORM (*Dates of composition are given in brackets.*)

1. *Révolte dans les Asturies. Essai de création collective.* (Play) (1935) Published in Algiers in 1936.

2. *L'Envers et l'Endroit* (Essays) (1935-36) Charlot, Algiers 1936.

3. *Noces* (Essays) (1936-37) Charlot, Algiers 1938. Reprinted by Gallimard, Paris 1945.

4. *L'Étranger* (*Récit*) (1939-40) Gallimard 1942. Translated into English by Stuart Gilbert, Preface by Cyril Connolly, Hamish Hamilton 1946. New edition, 1957.

5. *Le Mythe de Sisyphe* (*Essai sur l'absurde*) (1940-41) Gallimard 1942. Translated by Justin O'Brien, Hamish Hamilton 1955. (The same volume includes a number of essays in translation, 'Helen's Exile', 'The Minotaur or the Stop at Oran', etc.)

6. *Lettres à un ami allemand* (Letters) (1942-44) First published in book form in 1945. Gallimard.

7. *Le Malentendu* and *Caligula* (Plays) Written in 1943 and 1938, and produced in 1944 and 1945 respectively. Published together in book form in 1945. Translated by Stuart Gilbert, Hamish Hamilton 1947.

8. *La Peste* (*Chronique*) (1943-47) Gallimard 1947. Translated by Stuart Gilbert, Hamish Hamilton 1948.

9. *L'État de Siège* (Play) (1948) First produced 1948. Printed by Gallimard 1948.

10. *Les Justes* (Play) (1948-49) First produced 1950. Published in book form 1950. Gallimard.

11. *Actuelles I* and *Actuelles II* (Collections of political articles). Published in 1950 and 1953 respectively by Gallimard. The articles reprinted in these two volumes were originally written between 1944 and 1953.

12. *L'Homme révolté* (Essay) (1945-51) Gallimard 1951. Translated by Anthony Bower, with a preface by Sir Herbert Read, Hamish Hamilton, 1953.

13. *L' Été* (Essays) Published by Gallimard 1954. The essays reprinted in this volume were written between 1939 and 1953.

14. *La Chute* (*Récit*) (1955-56) Gallimard 1956. Translated by Justin O'Brien, Hamish Hamilton 1957.
15. *L'Exil et le Royaume* (Stories written between 1953-57) Gallimard 1957.

(B) ESSAYS, ETC., *published separately, as part of collections or in reviews*

1. *L'Espoir et l'Absurde dans l'Oeuvre de Franz Kafka.* *L'Arbalète*, 1943. Reprinted in augmented edition of *Le Mythe de Sisyphe*, 1945.
2. *Portrait d'un Élu. Les Cahiers du Sud*, April 1943, pp. 306-311.
3. *Sur une Philosophie de l'Expression. Poésie* 1944, January, pp. 15-23.
4. *La Remarque sur la Révolte*. 1945. Published in the collection *Existence* by Gallimard. Preface by Jean Grenier.
5. *Préface à une Anthologie de l'Insignifiance. Almanach des lettres et des arts*, Summer 1945.
6. *Les Meurtriers délicats. La Table Ronde*, No. 1, 1948. Reproduced in *L'Homme révolté*.
7. *Le Meurtre et l'Absurde. Empédocle*, No. 1, 1949.
8. *Nietzsche et le Nihilisme. Les Temps Modernes*, August 1951, pp. 88-97.
9. *Lautréamont et la Banalité. Les Cahiers du Sud*, No. 307, 1951, pp. 399-405. These articles were reproduced in *L'Homme révolté*.
10. *Rencontres avec André Gide. Hommage à André Gide.* N.R.F. 1951, pp. 223-228.

PREFACES

1. Chamfort. *Maximes et Anecdotes*. Preface by Camus. Monaco 1944.
2. André Salvet. *Le Combat silencieux*. Le Portulan 1945. (A novel on the Resistance movement) Preface by Camus.
3. René Leynaud. *Poésies Posthumes*. Gallimard 1947. Preface by Camus.
4. Jacques Méry. *Laissez passer mon Peuple*. Éditions du Seuil, 1947. Preface by Camus attacking the European attitude towards the Jews. Preface reproduced in *Actuelles II*.
5. Jeanne Héon-Canonne. *Devant la Mort*. Paris 1951. (A novel about the Resistance) Preface by Camus.
6. Daniel Mauriac. *Contre-Amour*. Éditions de Minuit. 1952. Preface by Camus.

7. A. Rosmer. *Moscou sous Lénine. Les Origines du Communisme.* Paris 1953. Preface by Camus.
8. Louis Guilloux. *La Maison du Peuple.* Grasset 1953. Preface by Camus.
9. Oscar Wilde. *La Ballade de la Géôle de Reading* (translated 1953). Preface by Camus entitled *L'Artiste en Prison.*
10. Bieber. *L'Allemagne vue par les Écrivains de la Résistance française.* Geneva and Lille, 1954. Preface by Camus.
11. Roger Martin du Gard. *Oeuvres.* Bibliothèque de la Pléiade 1955. Preface by Camus.

CRITICISM OF CAMUS'S WORK

An enormous number of articles have been published on Camus since 1945, and it is impossible to hope to give a complete bibliography. Nevertheless, the following should be noted.

(A) Four studies of Camus, in book form, published in French.

1. Léon Thoorens. *À la rencontre d'Albert Camus.* Brussels 1946.
2. Robert de Luppé. *Albert Camus.* Presses Universitaires 1951.
3. Albert Maquet. *Albert Camus ou l'invincible Été.* Carrefour des Lettres. Éditions Debresse 1955.
4. Roger Quilliot. *La Mer et les Prisons. Essai sur Albert Camus.* Gallimard 1956.

These last two studies both contain extensive bibliographies of French criticism of Camus.

(B) In English, the most important articles on Camus so far have been:

1. A. J. Ayer. *Novelist-Philosophers. Horizon,* March 1946.
2. Rayner Heppenstall. *Albert Camus and the Romantic Protest. Penguin New Writing,* No. 34, 1948, pp. 104-116.
3. Germaine Brée. *Introduction to Albert Camus. French Studies,* No. 1, 1950, pp. 27-37.
4. S. John. *Image and Symbol in Albert Camus. French Studies,* January 1955, pp. 42-53.
5. Richard Wollheim. *The Political Philosophy of Existentialism. Cambridge Journal,* October 1953, pp. 3-19.
6. H. R. Stockwell. *Albert Camus. Cambridge Journal,* August 1954, pp. 690-704.
7. Leon Roth. *Albert Camus. Philosophy,* October 1955, pp. 291-303.
8. J. Cruikshank. *Camus' Technique in 'L'Étranger'. French Studies,* Autumn 1955.

A Selected List of Evergreen Books

E306 **THE NEW BOOK/A BOOK OF TORTURE** — McClure — $1.95
E307 **RED EYE OF LOVE** — Weinstein — $1.75
E309 **ESSAYS IN ZEN BUDDHISM** — Suzuki — $2.95
E310 **PROBLEMS OF HISTORICAL PSYCHOLOGY** — Barbu — $1.95
E312 **SERJEANT MUSGRAVE'S DANCE** — Arden — $1.75
E315 **THE BIRTHDAY PARTY & THE ROOM** — Pinter — $1.75
E317 **F'INGS AIN'T WOT THEY USED T'BE** — Norman — $1.75
E318 **HAPPY DAYS** — Beckett — $1.45
E319 **CAPITAL PUNISHMENT** — Joyce — $1.95
E320 **LAST YEAR AT MARIENBAD** — Robbe-Grillet — $1.95
E321 **FEMALE SEXUALITY** — Bonaparte — $1.95
E322 **RITUAL** — Reik — $2.45
E324 **THE FUTURE AS HISTORY** — Heilbroner — $1.75
E325 **ONE WAY PENDULUM** — Simpson — $1.75
E326 **THANK YOU AND OTHER POEMS** — Koch — $1.95
E327 **DOCK BRIEF AND OTHER PLAYS** — Mortimer — $1.95
E328 **THE PALM-WINE DRINKARD** — Tutuola — $1.45
E329 **LYRICS OF THE MIDDLE AGES** — Creekmore — $2.95
E332 **MUNTU: AN OUTLINE OF THE NEW AFRICAN CULTURE** — Jahn — $2.45
E333 **BID ME TO LIVE** — H. D. — $1.95
E334 **MODERN GERMAN DRAMA** — Garten — $2.45
E336 **SAMUEL BECKETT** — Kenner — $1.95
E338 **THE LION IN LOVE** — Delaney — $1.75
E343 **MOSCOW REHEARSALS** — Houghton — $2.45
E344 **THE VISIT** — Durrenmatt — $1.75
E345 **HEROES OF THE GREEKS** — Kerenyi — $2.95
E347 **PSYCHOTHERAPY IN THE SOVIET UNION** — Winn — $1.95
E350 **THREE PLAYS** — Pinter — $1.95
E351 **THE ART OF MAKING DANCES** — Humphrey — $1.95
E352 **PARAPSYCHOLOGY** — Sudre — $2.95
E353 **FRIGIDITY IN WOMEN, VOL. I** — Stekel — $1.95
E354 **FRIGIDITY IN WOMEN, VOL. II** — Stekel — $1.95
E355 **PRESCRIPTION FOR REBELLION** — Lindner — $1.95
E356 **PSYCHOANALYSIS & CIVILIZATION** — Hollitscher — $1.45
E358 **INTRODUCTION TO MODERN EXISTENTIALISM** — Breisach — $2.45
E359 **THE LABYRINTH OF SOLITUDE** — Paz — $1.95
E360 **ZEN BUDDHISM & PSYCHOANALYSIS** — Suzuki, Fromm, DeMartino — $1.95
E362 **SADISM AND MASOCHISM, VOL. I** — Stekel — $2.95
E363 **SADISM AND MASOCHISM, VOL. II** — Stekel — $2.95
E364 **SELECTED POEMS OF PABLO NERUDA** — Belitt, trans. — $2.95
E365 **ARSHILE GORKY** — Rosenberg — $2.95
E368 **FICCIONES** — Borges — $2.45
E370 **EDUCATION FOR FREEDOM** — Hutchins — $1.45
E372 **MOTHER COURAGE** — Brecht — $1.95
E373 **HITLER'S SECRET BOOK** — $2.45
E374 **THE SCREENS** — Genet — $1.95
E375 **HELEN IN EGYPT** — H. D. — $2.45
E377 **MODERN GERMAN POETRY** — Hamburger, Middleton, eds. — $2.95
E378 **FILM: BOOK 2** — Hughes, ed. — $2.45
E379 **POEMS IN ENGLISH** — Beckett — $1.45
E380 **THE PHYSICISTS** — Durrenmatt — $1.75
E381 **TOM JONES** — Osborne — $1.95
E382 **STAND UP, FRIEND, WITH ME** — Field — $1.45
E383 **TOWARD JAZZ** — Hodeir — $1.95
E384 **SYSTEMATIC SOCIOLOGY** — Mannheim — $1.75

If your bookseller doesn't have these **Evergreen Books**, you may order them by writing to EVERGREEN BOOKS, Order Dept., 80 University Pl., New York 3, N. Y. Please enclose cash or money order, and add 25c for postage and handling.